WHAT COLOR IS YOUR PARACHUTE?
FOR TEENS

SECOND EDITION

WHAT COLOR IS YOUR PARACHUTE?
FOR TEENS

Discovering Yourself, Defining Your Future

Carol Christen and Richard N. Bolles

with *Jean M. Blomquist*

TEN SPEED PRESS
Berkeley

This book is dedicated to my mother, Muriel Christen-Jones. People like her and my step-father, Bill Jones, have my complete admiration. They have overcome circumstance and early bad decisions to thrive and have persevered to create a life they love. You go, Mom!

Published in the United States by Ten Speed Press, an imprint of the Crown Publishing Group, a division of Random House, Inc., New York.
www.crownpublishing.com
www.tenspeed.com

Ten Speed Press and the Ten Speed Press colophon are registered trademarks of Random House, Inc.

The Library of Congress has cataloged the first edition as follows:

Bolles, Richard Nelson.
  What color is your parachute? for teens : discovering yourself, defining your future / Richard Nelson Bolles and Carol Christen, with Jean M. Blomquist.
      p. cm.
  Includes bibliographical references and index.
  ISBN-13: 978-1-58008-713-1 (alk. paper)
  ISBN-10: 1-58008-713-2 (alk. paper)
  1. Teenagers—Vocational guidance. 2. Job hunting. I. Christen, Carol.
II. Blomquist, Jean M. III. Title.
  HF5381.B63513 2006
  331.702083'5—dc22

                              2006005029

ISBN 978-1-58008-141-2

Illustration on pages 74–75 by Ann Miya
Front cover photograph copyright © Image Source/Getty Images
Back cover photograph copyright © Rob Melnychuk/Digital Vision/Getty Images
Cover and text design by Betsy Stromberg

Printed in the United States of America

10 9

Revised Edition

MY PARACHUTE

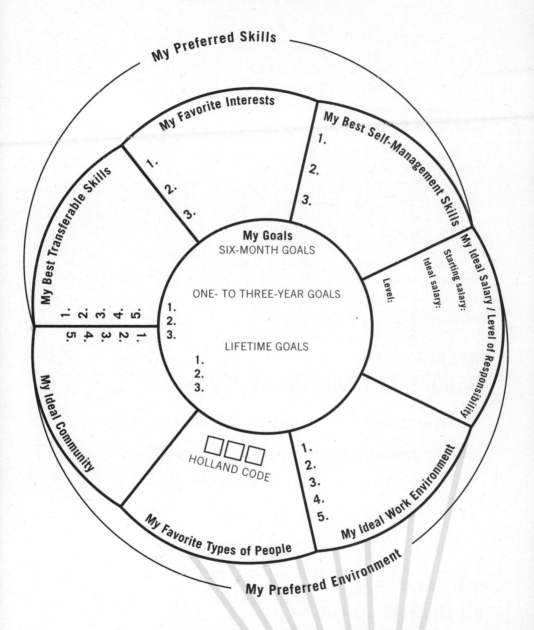

To make this form easier
to use, photocopy this page
and enlarge it.

CONTENTS

ACKNOWLEDGMENTS

Bouquets of thanks to all who helped with this book, especially the following:

Phil Wood, for calling to ask about my interest in adapting *Parachute* for teens. Richard N. Bolles, for writing the original *What Color Is Your Parachute?* and enabling millions of people—myself included—to find jobs and careers they love. Winifred Wood, for issuing the challenge that planted the seeds for this book. Lily Binns, editor of the first edition, and Lisa Westmoreland, second edition editor; both have extraordinary skills at herding cats and authors. Lisa plays excellent manuscript Frisbee and is such fun to work with. Kristi Hein for her amazing copyediting (I am in awe of her skills). Betsy Stromberg, art director, for her cool cover and interior design. The entire team at Ten Speed/ Random House that designs, produces, publicizes, markets, sells, and ships this book. Together we've created a wonderful career resource for teens. Colleagues Jim Cassio, Sue Cullen, Rich Feller, Tanya Gilbert, Letta Hlavachek, Jim Kell, Tom Jackson, Brian McIvor, Marty Nemko, Daniel Porot, Patti Wilson, and Robin Roman Wright for giving me helpful suggestions and access to their brilliant minds. David Maxwell, chair of the business department at Ernest Righetti High School; Jeff Stein and Matt Aydelott of the workforce development projects at Cuesta College; and Professor Jim Howland of the Technical/ Professional Writing Program at Cal Poly, San Luis Obispo, for allowing me access to their students. The hundreds of teens and young adults who shared their learnings, hopes, and fears. Cynthia Campbell, for being such a caring friend and psychic about when to call. Muriel Christen-Jones, my mother, for her unconditional support of this project, and me. Dr. Serena Brewer, my daughter, for her encouragement (leap . . . and the net will appear), brainstorming, giving me access to her worldwide network, and, most important, taking the time to find a career path she loves. Finally, huge thanks to my best friend and loving husband, Joe Risser, for endless cups of tea, being a sturdy wall against which to bounce ideas, and keeping CR Farms going while I was otherwise engaged. Your love is my safety net.

With deep gratitude,
Carol Christen

PREFACE TO THE SECOND EDITION, OR HOW CAN THIS BOOK HELP ME?

Welcome to the adventure of your life.

Wait, isn't this book about choosing a career? Yes, but before you can start making decisions about careers, you really need to think out the life you want and what work will help you get that life. What purpose do you want your life to serve? What purpose does work serve in your life?

This book can help you answer those questions. By reading this book and doing the exercises, you will learn how to describe the life you want as a young adult (or beyond), what you want in a dream job, and how to use that information to help you identify the training, education, and jobs that will help you get the experience and skills you need to qualify for your dream job.

Work you will enjoy grows out of your values—that is, what is important to you. This book has been written to help you learn, step by step, what values are important to you and what kind of a life you want. That way, you'll be able to describe what makes up a job that is good for you and how to go about getting hired to do work you want to do.

We know you don't really want to read a book. You're asking, "Isn't there some quicker method of learning what kind of career is right for me?" It would be so much easier if there were a foolproof method for helping each teen discover their perfect job. It would be lovely if there were a "sorting hat" for careers. Put it on your head and instead of saying which Hogwarts house you belong to, it would tell you what job was perfect for you. But there really isn't one perfect job that, if you're lucky enough to guess right, you'll have forever. What's perfect for you will change with age, experience, and the economy.

Like the Knights of the Round Table, you have a quest. Except, instead of finding the holy grail, your quest is to find your place in the world, what kind of a life you want, and how you are going to earn a living in ways you can enjoy. Most teens want their adult years to be fun and fulfilling—which is hard to achieve if you hate your job.

As fascinating as you are, it can take a while to get to know yourself and to pull information about you and the world of work together. In studying young adult success in transitioning from school to work, it's surprising to find that it takes about ten years to get from no clue, to a detailed plan, to well-employed. So if you hope to spend your quarterlife birthday celebrating your personal and professional success, plan on beginning your career exploration about age fifteen.

Why fifteen? There are lots of reasons, but the most compelling is that you've still got plenty of time to become aware of dozens of careers, check them out, toss some out, find some more to explore, and eventually find several options that really interest you. In addition, planning ahead gives you time to take classes that will improve your employment skills or let you go deeper into subjects you like.

If you're just fifteen, you can skip the first four chapters (for now). Read them when you're seventeen or eighteen. Those chapters are for older teens with some work experience, and teach you how to find your favorite interests, skills, and goals to create a description of what you want in a job. We suggest you start reading this book at the end. Chapter 12 is about the life you want as a twentysomething, which

CREATE YOUR OWN CAREER CLASS

If your school doesn't have a career class, get a few ambitious friends together and create your own *Careers* book club or *Introduction to Career Planning* course. In addition to this book, here is my recommended bibliography:

Getting Real: Helping Teens Find Their Futures by Kenneth C. Gray

Luck Is No Accident: Making the Most of Happenstance in Your Life and Career by John Krumboltz and Al Levin

Make Things Happen: The Key to Networking for Teens by Lara Zielin

If you are considering going to college, you should also read:

Generation Broke by Anya Kemenetz

Major in Success by Patrick Combs

is a good goal to start thinking about now! You might also want to check out How to Find What You Love to Do: Naming Your Interests (chapter 1, page 10) and the Party exercise (chapter 2, page 23) to get ideas about career fields to explore.

Fifteen is a good age to ask yourself the following question: *"Is it important to me to be able to choose and shape the life and work I do, or am I willing to take what's available?"* If you want to choose and shape your life, you'll have a great adventure. But first you'll have to learn some new skills for making decisions. This book will introduce you to those skills. Like learning any new set of skills, you'll get better at them the more you use them.

If having the life you want or working at a particular job is your definition of the good life, we recommend that by the time you reach age seventeen you read this book—and do the exercises—from cover to cover. By your senior year (or before, if you're the plan-way-ahead type), you should have come up with well-researched strategies for achieving your work and personal goals. What's important is not the job you pick—it's learning the process of how to pick one. After all, most adults have quite a few jobs before they find their dream job.

Jobs are like clothing; you have to try on a lot of them before you begin to find your style and outfits that fit you well. And, like the world of fashion, the job market is constantly changing. Some jobs that were in "fashion" a decade ago may not even exist today. Jobs you'll love in your thirties and forties may not exist today. Many students pick a dream job and as they work toward it, they find jobs they like even better. No wonder you want to start this process now, in high school. It takes young people about a decade to wrestle with these issues, make some initial decisions, and find where they fit in the world of work. The sooner you start, the sooner you'll get the life you want.

Older than fifteen and you haven't done any career exploration or planning? Don't despair. Just read this book and catch up. Learning what you want and designing a career plan will help you no matter what your age.

We're delighted to have had a chance to update this book. The economy has changed, and so has the job market. Finding a job is tougher than ever—according to the National Association of Colleges and Employers, just 20 percent of last year's college grads have found full-time jobs. But if you know what fascinates you, and you continue to develop and revise your career plans, you'll be better prepared than other job applicants when the time comes to get hired! In addition, we wanted to offer you the very latest in ideas, tools, statistics, and resources that can help you discover the life you want and great jobs to fund that life.

GET IN TOUCH!

Thanks to all who have written to us sharing your experiences with the first edition of the book. Authors love to hear from their readers. Your stories help make later editions better. If you would like to share your experiences using this book, your thoughts on creating a life or career you love, or a good resource (book or website), please email Carol Christen at carol@carolchristen.com. You can track developing career issues and Carol's latest research at her blog: www.parachute4teens.com/blog.html. You can also contact Richard Bolles, and access his blog, through his website: www.jobhuntersbible.com.

INTRODUCTION

This book is about you—and your future—which is, of course, a very fascinating subject! We want to explore who you are, what's important to you, and what you like to do. Why? We believe life is meant to be lived to the fullest, and we want to give you the tools to create the kind of life you want. We want to help you discover what you'd love to do with your life, especially work that you will love.

"But I'm only fourteen [or fifteen, sixteen, seventeen, eighteen]," you say. "I'm too young to be thinking about my life's work!" We agree. We don't expect you to plan out your whole career in high school, or even in college. This book is to help you create your first career path. Your first career path is simply how you want to earn a living as a young adult when you leave school, at whatever level that is. The sooner you start thinking about your future, the more time you have to explore all your options.

We think your teen years are a great time to be thinking about your life's work. For many, high school may be the only time you have enough time to check out all the jobs that match your interests. Although this can be done when you are living on your own, it's so much easier to do while your parents are paying your bills! As a young adult, you're beginning to discover what's important to you—how you like to spend your time, who you like to be with, which classes interest you (and which ones don't). And most likely, you're becoming aware that some adults you know—teachers, parents, coaches, and others—really enjoy what they're doing, and others don't. We want to help you find work that you'll enjoy—work that's fun, satisfying, and challenging, all rolled into one.

Who Should Read This Book?

Whether college-bound or work-bound after high school, this book is for you if any of the following describe you:

- You care about how you'll earn a living.

- You have career goals but may not know how to reach them.

- You want to find a college major that's right for you.

- You want to take as much control over your life as possible.

- You hope to become financially independent as soon as possible.

- You hope to find a fun job to finance your life while you figure out what you really want to do for work, what kind of a life you want to have and how you can get that life, and who, as a person, you really want to be.

In short, if you want work that you love, enjoy, or feel is the right fit for you, and if you're willing to spend some time learning about yourself and about the world of work, this book is for you.

Why Do I Need This Book?

Finding a job you'll love takes not only time and energy but also awareness of many kinds of careers, plus career-choice and job-search skills. Chances are, even if you feel like you're quite busy now, you have time and energy you can devote to increasing your awareness of what kind of work is good for you, and gaining skills that will help you find that kind of work. When we talked with young adults engaged in their own job hunt, they often told us that if they had only known how to use their time in school to make themselves more employable in the future, they would have made better use of that time.

Both authors of this book have websites through which they hear from job hunters around the world. They often receive letters from people who say they have been surprised by how hard it has been to find a job, or how long it has taken them.Too many young people use techniques they've heard mentioned over the years. Unfortunately, today's economy is too tricky to rely on hearsay techniques. Getting a challenging job that pays well and interests you isn't easy. Studying the effective job-search and career development techniques outlined in this book will greatly improve your chances of getting hired for jobs you really want.

We want you to be prepared, not surprised. We want to help you to work smart, which means developing job-search savvy that will help you now and throughout your adult life. If you use your time now to do some planning for how you want to earn a living, you stand a good chance of achieving your career goals. Even if you're not sure what you want to do—and you're not alone there (many adults feel that way too)—we'll help you discover just what kind of job will be a good and satisfying one for you. You'll learn what you need to know about yourself and about the world of work so that you can make good choices about how you want to live and work.

Why Did We Write This Book?

We want you to find work that you love or build a life you love through work you enjoy. We want to give you the skills necessary to find out what it is you love to do, and to find a job where you can do just that.

In our work, we meet thousands of adults who don't know how to find work they love. When they were in high school, very few of them learned effective job-search skills—usually because classes in job-search skills weren't even offered. Even though adults are expected to work, few have been taught how to discover what they most wanted out of work and life, or what employers wanted and expected of them. Of

> **REALITY CHECK**
>
> You can do an amazing amount of career work, including reading this book, in just twenty minutes a day.

those students planning on college, many don't receive guidance on selecting a major, even though finding the right major is an important step toward finding a great job.

We want your life to be different. We want you to have both the skills and the knowledge necessary to find good and rewarding work throughout your life.

The world of work changes constantly. Some jobs disappear, while new ones appear; others change significantly because of scientific advances, new technology, or the needs and expectations of society. The strength or weakness of the economy also affects the number and types of jobs available. If you have solid job-search skills and know what you really want to do, you can thrive—or, like a cat, always land on your feet—even when the work world changes.

Perhaps you've had a few part-time jobs already. Maybe you liked your work, maybe you didn't. More likely, you liked some parts of your work but not others. Those work experiences—and all your life experiences—are valuable because they can tell you important things about yourself and about the work you want to do.

Are you ready for an adventure? Great! That's what this book can offer you—an adventure in discovering more about you and what's most important to you. So let's get started by looking at your life and discovering your answer to this question: How do I find work I will love?

WHAT CAREER PLANNING IS—AND ISN'T

Some people think that career planning means narrowing down your options or making a decision early and being stuck with it. Good career planning—the kind you're going to learn by reading this book—doesn't do either. In fact, Parachute career planning is a decision-making process that involves learning about yourself and the job market so you can expand—not narrow—your options.

PART ONE

DISCOVERING YOUR DREAM JOB

Hold on to those dreams of being a firefighter or ship captain or doctor or nurse. Don't let others tell you that those are silly dreams. I think so many people end up doing, consciously or not, what others expect of them, or they settle for less because they think achieving their dream is too hard.

—ROB SANDERS,
pediatric physician, age 28

DO you know what your dream job is? If you have talked with half a dozen people who do that job and you're absolutely sure of what you long to do, that's great. But maybe you aren't so sure. That's fine too. Perhaps your dream job will become clear over time, as it does for many people. Whichever is true for you, we believe that the search for your dream job is very important. Because so much of your adult life will be spent working, finding work you love will help make your whole life more satisfying, gratifying, and fun.

Speaking of fun, that's what the process of finding your dream job can be. You'll become a detective looking for clues in your own life, discovering what matters most to you: what you love to do, who your favorite types of people are, and where you'd like to do what you love to do. As you gather together these clues from your own life, you'll discover the foundation for finding work you love.

Most people don't find their dream job because they think that having their whole dream come true isn't possible. They may pursue just part of it—whatever they think might come true. The problem is, if you only pursue half your dream, your whole heart won't be in it. You'll pursue that half dream half-heartedly, and half your dream is all that will ever come true.

"I was lucky—I found what I wanted to do early in life."

—STEVE JOBS, cofounder and CEO of Apple

We want you to discover and pursue your whole dream with your whole heart! To do this, we'll begin by asking you three basic questions in part 1 of this book: What do you like to do and what are you good at? Who (that is, what kind of people) do you like to do those things with? Where do you like to do those things? Once you know your what, who, and where, you'll be ready to explore how to find work you'll love. We'll look at the question of *how* in part 3. But before that, in part 2 we'll look at some things you can do right now to get yourself on your way to your dream job.

Before you begin your detective work, though, you may have one other question you'd like answered: Why is this book called *What Color Is Your Parachute? For Teens*? The "for teens" part is clear—it means this book is for you. But what about this "parachute" thing? We use the image of a parachute because a parachute helps you land where you want and need to land. In the case of finding your dream job, your parachute is made up of all your skills, goals, and desires or dreams. Everyone's parachute is a different color because every person's skills, goals, and desires come together in a different way. As you explore the questions what, who, and where (and how, in part 3), you'll list your most important discoveries about yourself on your own parachute (see My Parachute diagram, page v).

You may want to keep your answers in a journal and return to these questions after a few months, after your first job, or after you get some technical training or go on to college. Your answers will change as you accumulate more life and work experience. The answers to some questions may not be very clear now, but they'll become clearer over time. And answers that you're certain of now may remain steady through the years, which will confirm their importance in your life.

When you put all your what, who, and where clues in one place (on your parachute), you'll have a clear word picture to guide you in finding work you'll love. Whatever color it is, your parachute will be designed to help you land in just the right spot in life—in a job you'll love.

1

What You Love to Do

YOUR FAVORITE INTERESTS AND BEST SKILLS

Why does this first chapter focus on what you love to do? Because what you love to do reveals your interests and your skills. Those favorite interests and skills, especially the skills that you most enjoy using (which we call your "best" skills), are major clues to finding work that you'll love. Let's look at your interests first.

Discover Your Favorite Interests

Take a moment and think about how you spend your time. Of the things that you do, what is the most fun? What captures your attention—and your imagination? What is your favorite subject in school? Everyone will have different answers—his or her unique combination of interests. Danika, for example, loves movies. Jeff spends hours on his computer, trying to figure out new ways of doing things. Jessica loves plants and gardening, and Darnel lives and breathes sports—all kinds of sports. So how might these different interests lead Danika, Jeff, Jessica, and Darnel to work they'll love?

Let's take a look at Danika's interests first. She loves movies. If she chooses movies (or filmmaking) as a career field, what could she do? Our first thoughts usually go to the obvious: she could be an actress, a screenwriter, or a director—or maybe a movie critic (then she'd get to see lots of movies). But Danika has many more possibilities to choose from. She could be a researcher (especially for historical movies), travel expert (to scout locations), interior designer (to design sets), carpenter (to build sets), painter (for backdrops and the like), costume designer, makeup artist, hair stylist, camera operator, lighting technician, sound mixer or editor, composer (for soundtracks), stunt person, caterer, personal assistant (to the director or cast members), first aid person, secretary, publicist, accountant, or any number of other things.

Danika also loves animals and is really good at training them. She could combine her interests—movies and animals—with her skill in training animals, and become an animal trainer (or "wrangler" as they're sometimes called) for the film industry. That's a job most people wouldn't think of when considering careers in film.

What kind of career might Jeff's interest in computers lead to? He could be a programmer, do computer repair, or develop video games. Or because he loves art as well as computers, maybe he'll work with Danika in the film industry as a computer graphics designer (for special effects).

Jessica, because of her interest in plants and gardening, could become a florist, botanist, or developer of plant hybrids, or she might run her own landscape design, lawn maintenance, or plant nursery business. Darnel's love of sports might lead him to be a professional athlete, a coach, or maybe—because he loves working with kids and has a little brother with cerebral palsy—he might teach adaptive physical education, helping children with physical disabilities get the exercise they need.

As you can see, your interests can lead you in many different directions in your work life. It's true that interests change with time, age, and exposure to new people, places, and experiences. But it's also true that your interests now may be with you all your life, so naming your current interests is a great starting place for finding work you'll love. Let's take a closer look at your interests now.

HOW TO FIND WHAT YOU LOVE TO DO: NAMING YOUR INTERESTS

Write your answer to each question on a slip of paper or sticky note.

- When you've got free time, what do you like to do?
- What's your favorite subject in school?
- When you're in the magazine section of your school library or a bookstore, what type of magazine (computer, fashion, sports, and so forth) will you pick up and read first?
- Fill in the blank: When I'm _____, I lose track of time and don't want anyone or anything to disturb me.
- If someone asked you what your favorite interests are, what would you say?
- What are your favorite hobbies, sports, or recreational activities?
- What Internet sites do you have bookmarked? What is the subject matter of those sites?
- What kinds of problems do you like to solve?
- What kinds of questions do your friends or classmates bring to you for help?

After you've answered all the questions, put your answers in a list. Use sticky notes (or experiment with a prioritizing grid at www.groundofyourownchoosing.com/grid. htm) to make a new list in order of priority (your favorite interest first, second favorite next, and so on). Then write your top three interests in the My Favorite Interests section of My Parachute (page v). If your interests change, be sure to update your parachute.

Good work! You're off to a great start.

Skills You Enjoy Using

Your interests are closely tied to your skills, especially the skills that you most enjoy using. We call these your "best" skills because they are your best bet to finding a job that you love. How? It's simple: when you know what your skills are, especially your best skills, you can look for jobs that use those particular skills. It just makes sense that the jobs you are most likely to enjoy will use your favorite skills. Once hired, you're more likely to keep your job if it involves your interests and skills you do well. Why? To succeed in most fields, you have to work long hours. It's hard to succeed if you don't like what you do. You'll want to spend less time at work, not more.

"But I don't have any skills," you say.

Chances are you have more skills than you realize. Often our best skills are so close to us that we're not even aware of them. They come so easily and naturally that we think anybody can do them the way we do. It's true that you probably don't have as many skills as your older brother or sister has, and they probably don't have as many skills as your parents or favorite teachers have. Skills grow as we grow.

As we gain more life experience, pursue further education, or work at a particular job for an extended period of time, we also gain more skills. But by the time you're a teenager, you've already developed many skills.

Transferable Skills

At its most basic, a skill is a developed aptitude or ability. A skill can range from a basic life skill like being able to turn on a water faucet (which we can't do till we're tall enough to reach the faucet and strong enough to turn the handle) to a more advanced skill like being able to drive a car. (Skills are sometimes called "talents" or "gifts." In this book, we'll use the word "skills.")

There are many different types of skills, and the most basic are transferable skills. Along with your interests, transferable skills are the foundation for knowing what you love to do. Sometimes they're also called "functional" skills because these are skills you do,

> **REALITY CHECK**
>
> It takes a long time to get good at something. You might as well spend that time involved with something that really interests you. Many successful ventures—such as RoadtripNation, Facebook, and Playing for Change—were started by young entrepreneurs following their interests.

such as gathering information or data, or working with people or things. Let's say you like to skateboard. (Skateboarding could be one of the interests you named earlier.) When you skateboard, you work with some "thing" (a skateboard), and skateboarding is what you do with the skateboard. What are your transferable skills? You have hand–eye–foot coordination, physical agility, and exceptional balance, as well as the ability to make split-second decisions and take risks. Nothing limits these skills to skateboarding. They'd be valuable in (that is, transferable to) work as a surfing instructor, lumberjack, search-and-rescue crew member, or any number of other jobs.

Transferable skills can be divided into three different types: physical, mental, and interpersonal. Physical skills primarily use the hands and/or body and generally involve working with things (such as materials, equipment, or objects, like your skateboard). Working with things includes working with nature (plants and animals). Mental skills primarily use the mind and generally involve working with data, information, numbers, or ideas. Interpersonal skills primarily involve working with people as you serve or help them with their needs or problems. (We call these different types of skills "Skill TIPs"—that is, skills that you use when working with Things, Information/Ideas, or People.) So if one of your skills is skateboarding, your transferable skills include physical skills (hand-eye-foot coordination, agility, balance, and skateboard maneuvering) and mental skills (split-second decision making). Skateboarding can also involve using interpersonal skills, especially if you are on a team, enjoy teaching others how to skateboard, or do specialized tricks and maneuvers.

Why Are My Transferable Skills Important?

Your transferable skills are particularly important as you look for your dream job because they can be transferred from one place to another, to any field or career you choose, regardless of where you first picked them up or how long you've had them. For example, your ability to swim is a skill that can be transferred to—or used in—work as a lifeguard, a swim coach, or a counselor at a summer camp.

DISCOVERY EXERCISE

HOW TO FIND WHAT YOU LOVE TO DO: IDENTIFYING YOUR SKILLS

You begin to identify your skills by looking at your life. Think about projects you have completed, recent problems that you solved, your hobbies, and the activities you do for fun. These can be experiences from your school, volunteer work, paid work, or free time. Select a project or activity you've enjoyed that had an outcome—writing a paper, helping to organize an activity, or learning something new, such as a sport or hobby.

Rich Feller, an international career consultant and author of the book *Knowledge Nomads and the Nervously Employed,* says that 70 percent of our skills come from challenges, 20 percent from watching others, and 10 percent from classes and reading. You may have stories to write from any of those three categories. But if you are stumped about what might make a good skills story, look particularly at challenges you have overcome. Once you've thought of a story, write a short paragraph that describes how you completed your project or worked out a solution to the problem you had.

Now give your project, problem, or activity a title. Then answer these questions:

- **Goal or Problem:** What was your goal—that is, what were you trying to accomplish, or what was the problem you were trying to solve?
- **Obstacles:** What made achieving your goal (or solving the problem) difficult? How did you overcome these obstacles?
- **Time Frame:** How long did it take you to achieve your goal or solve your problem?
- **Outcome:** What happened? Did things go as you expected, or did something unexpected happen?

Transferable skills are the basic building blocks of any job or career. Most jobs rely on just four to seven main skills. (These groups of skills are sometimes called "skill sets.") That's why it's so important to identify yours. If you know your best transferable skills, you can compare the skills needed in a job with those you do well and enjoy using. This kind of comparison will help you find a job you'll love. The more of your best skills you use in a job, the more likely you will love it.

Need a little inspiration on what kind of story to write? Serena Brewer was a seventeen-year-old high school senior when she wrote the following story.

MY COMMUNITY SERVICE PROJECT
By Serena Brewer • The Athenian School (Danville, CA)

The high school I attended required seniors to design and complete a community service project. My project stemmed from my love of teaching skiing and a unique opportunity that came from a phone call with my dad.

My dad was a school superintendent for a school district near the mountains. One of his schools offered alpine and cross-country skiing to fourth to eighth graders for P.E. credit. The school had a class for Down syndrome kids. I asked if the kids from this class got to go skiing. When my dad said no, I instantly knew what my community service project would be. Most kids who have this syndrome have enough motor coordination to participate in activities like skiing. I wanted to give these kids a chance to have fun in the snow and maybe even ski.

After overcoming his initial resistance, my dad put me in contact with the woman who taught the class for students with Down syndrome and with a family that might be willing to let me work with their kids. I created an outline of what we would do and how I would teach them. I met with the teacher and the family. I convinced the local ski resort to donate ski rentals and access to the rope tow and beginner's area. It turned out that the kids didn't remember much from one lesson to another. But they did experience something new and had fun.

> ### HOW DO TRANSFERABLE SKILLS HELP ME FIND MY DREAM JOB?
>
> Every job has certain core activities or tasks that you do over and over. To do these activities or tasks, you need to have certain skills. If you know what skills you most enjoy using, you'll be able to compare the skills needed in a job to your own best skills. If a job doesn't use three-quarters of your best skills, you won't be happy with it.

My high school was one of a group of schools around the world that empha-size community service. The head of my school submitted my project in a compe-tition. I was amazed when I was chosen to receive an international community service award for my project.

COMMUNITY SERVICE PROJECT

Goal or Problem: Designing a community service project to meet graduation requirements.
Obstacles: Convincing people that students with Down syndrome could learn to ski and enjoy the snow just like other elementary students; obtaining free ski rentals and ski passes.
Time Frame: Three months (January–March).
Outcome: Five Down syndrome students were able to experience skiing; community service award received.

Are you ready for a little detective work? Good! Let's turn to your life now and begin to identify your skills and, in particular, your best skills.

Discover Your Skills

Now that you've read My Community Service Project, reread your own story. Using the list of Skill TIPs (pages 16–18), identify the skills you use in your story. All of the skills in this list are transferable skills—skills that you can use in many different settings or jobs. You may want to photocopy the Skill TIPs list before you begin so you'll have a fresh copy to use if you want to do this exercise in the future or if you want to share it with a friend.

As you go through the Skill TIPs list, put a check mark in box #1 under each skill that you used in the story you just wrote. For example, if you used the skill "making" in your story (say, you made a dress or a sculpture), put a check mark in box #1 underneath "using my hands" on the Skills with Things page (page 16).

Here are a few of the skills that Serena, who wrote about her community service project, might have selected:

- Skills with Things (physical): motor/physical coordination with my whole body (skiing)

- Skills with Information (mental): imagining, inventing, creating, or designing new ideas (designing a skiing program for students with Down syndrome)

- Skills with People (interpersonal): teaching, training, or designing educational events (teaching skiing to students with Down syndrome and designing the program to teach them to ski)

Now that you've gone through the process and understand how it works, write four more stories so you have a total of five. If you wrote about a project the first time, try writing about something else: teaching your little sister how to ride a bike, learning to ice-skate, dealing with a friend who gossiped about you behind your back. Having five stories will help you find the different kinds of skills you use in different situations. You've already written story #1. Next, for story #2, place check marks in box #2 for each skill you used. Do this for each of the remaining stories, #3, #4, and #5. (If you want, brighten up the list by using colored pens or pencils.) You may find that in each story, you used many different skills—some in the "things" category, others in the "information" category, and still others in the "people" category. If you write one story a day and fill in your skills, then in five days you can know what your best transferable skills are—and you'll have two sections of your parachute done!

> **DISCOVER YOUR SKILLS**
>
> 1. Review your story.
> 2. Identify the skills you used.
> 3. Check your skills off on the Skill TIPs list (pages 16–18).

Identify Your Best Transferable Skills

Now we're ready to find which skills are your "best" ones—the ones you most enjoy using. Every job will include some tasks or need a few skills you don't much care for. But to find a job you'll enjoy, you want to know which skills you really like to use and which ones you do well. Think about big chunks of time. What skills do you like enough to use over and over all day long?

You have both "can-do" and "want-to" skills. Can-do skills are ones you don't want to use very often. For example, you probably have the skills to wash all the dishes from Thanksgiving dinner for thirty people. But how often would you want to use those skills—all day, every day, once a year, never?

Want-to skills are ones you enjoy using and could do over and over again, several times a day, and not go crazy. It's important to remember that each of us has different can-do and want-to skills. The world needs people with different skills.

SKILLS WITH THINGS

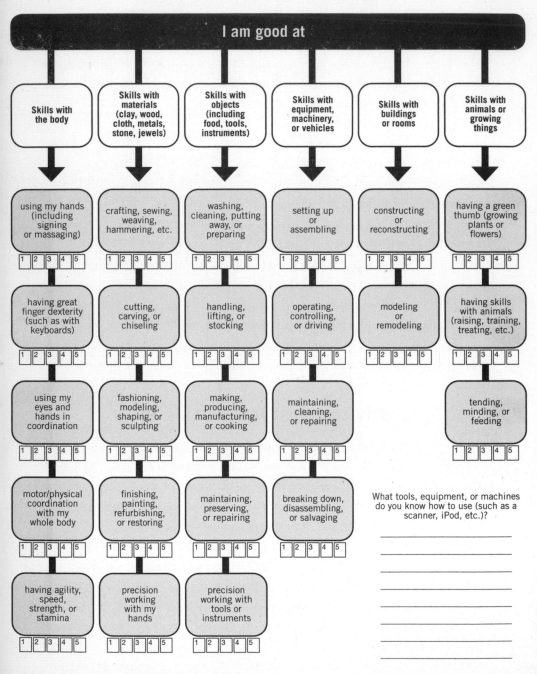

I am good at

Skills with the body → using my hands (including signing or massaging) `1 2 3 4 5` → having great finger dexterity (such as with keyboards) `1 2 3 4 5` → using my eyes and hands in coordination `1 2 3 4 5` → motor/physical coordination with my whole body `1 2 3 4 5` → having agility, speed, strength, or stamina `1 2 3 4 5`

Skills with materials (clay, wood, cloth, metals, stone, jewels) → crafting, sewing, weaving, hammering, etc. `1 2 3 4 5` → cutting, carving, or chiseling `1 2 3 4 5` → fashioning, modeling, shaping, or sculpting `1 2 3 4 5` → finishing, painting, refurbishing, or restoring `1 2 3 4 5` → precision working with my hands `1 2 3 4 5`

Skills with objects (including food, tools, instruments) → washing, cleaning, putting away, or preparing `1 2 3 4 5` → handling, lifting, or stocking `1 2 3 4 5` → making, producing, manufacturing, or cooking `1 2 3 4 5` → maintaining, preserving, or repairing `1 2 3 4 5` → precision working with tools or instruments `1 2 3 4 5`

Skills with equipment, machinery, or vehicles → setting up or assembling `1 2 3 4 5` → operating, controlling, or driving `1 2 3 4 5` → maintaining, cleaning, or repairing `1 2 3 4 5` → breaking down, disassembling, or salvaging `1 2 3 4 5`

Skills with buildings or rooms → constructing or reconstructing `1 2 3 4 5` → modeling or remodeling `1 2 3 4 5`

Skills with animals or growing things → having a green thumb (growing plants or flowers) `1 2 3 4 5` → having skills with animals (raising, training, treating, etc.) `1 2 3 4 5` → tending, minding, or feeding `1 2 3 4 5`

What tools, equipment, or machines do you know how to use (such as a scanner, iPod, etc.)?

_____
_____
_____
_____
_____
_____
_____
_____

SKILLS WITH INFORMATION

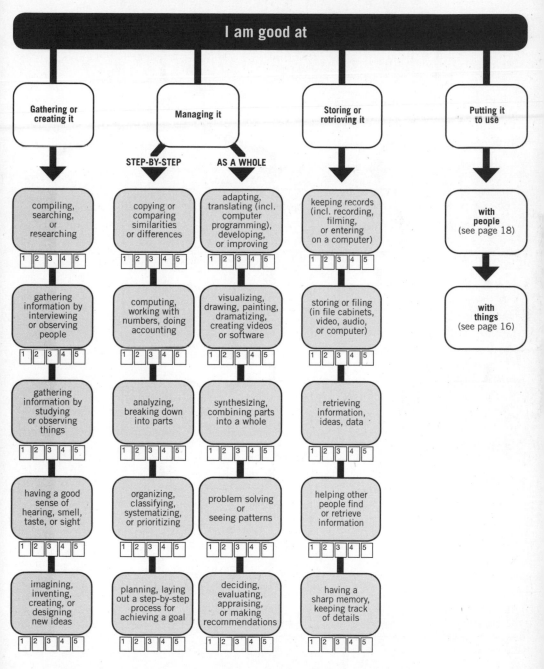

I am good at

Gathering or creating it

Managing it

Storing or rotrioving it

Putting it to use

STEP-BY-STEP   AS A WHOLE

Gathering or creating it	Managing it (STEP-BY-STEP)	Managing it (AS A WHOLE)	Storing or retrieving it	Putting it to use
compiling, searching, or researching	copying or comparing similarities or differences	adapting, translating (incl. computer programming), developing, or improving	keeping records (incl. recording, tilming, or entering on a computer)	**with people** (see page 18)
1 2 3 4 5	1 2 3 4 5	1 2 3 4 5	1 2 3 4 5	
gathering information by interviewing or observing people	computing, working with numbers, doing accounting	visualizing, drawing, painting, dramatizing, creating videos or software	storing or filing (in file cabinets, video, audio, or computer)	**with things** (see page 16)
1 2 3 4 5	1 2 3 4 5	1 2 3 4 5	1 2 3 4 5	
gathering information by studying or observing things	analyzing, breaking down into parts	synthesizing, combining parts into a whole	retrieving information, ideas, data	
1 2 3 4 5	1 2 3 4 5	1 2 3 4 5	1 2 3 4 5	
having a good sense of hearing, smell, taste, or sight	organizing, classifying, systematizing, or prioritizing	problem solving or seeing patterns	helping other people find or retrieve information	
1 2 3 4 5	1 2 3 4 5	1 2 3 4 5	1 2 3 4 5	
imagining, inventing, creating, or designing new ideas	planning, laying out a step-by-step process for achieving a goal	deciding, evaluating, appraising, or making recommendations	having a sharp memory, keeping track of details	
1 2 3 4 5	1 2 3 4 5	1 2 3 4 5	1 2 3 4 5	

SKILLS WITH PEOPLE

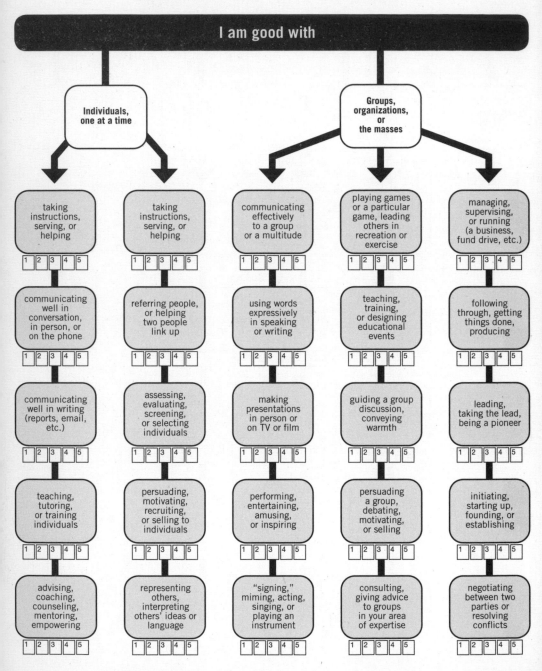

I am good with

Individuals, one at a time

Groups, organizations, or the masses

Individuals, one at a time		Groups, organizations, or the masses		
taking instructions, serving, or helping 1 2 3 4 5	taking instructions, serving, or helping 1 2 3 4 5	communicating effectively to a group or a multitude 1 2 3 4 5	playing games or a particular game, leading others in recreation or exercise 1 2 3 4 5	managing, supervising, or running (a business, fund drive, etc.) 1 2 3 4 5
communicating well in conversation, in person, or on the phone 1 2 3 4 5	referring people, or helping two people link up 1 2 3 4 5	using words expressively in speaking or writing 1 2 3 4 5	teaching, training, or designing educational events 1 2 3 4 5	following through, getting things done, producing 1 2 3 4 5
communicating well in writing (reports, email, etc.) 1 2 3 4 5	assessing, evaluating, screening, or selecting individuals 1 2 3 4 5	making presentations in person or on TV or film 1 2 3 4 5	guiding a group discussion, conveying warmth 1 2 3 4 5	leading, taking the lead, being a pioneer 1 2 3 4 5
teaching, tutoring, or training individuals 1 2 3 4 5	persuading, motivating, recruiting, or selling to individuals 1 2 3 4 5	performing, entertaining, amusing, or inspiring 1 2 3 4 5	persuading a group, debating, motivating, or selling 1 2 3 4 5	initiating, starting up, founding, or establishing 1 2 3 4 5
advising, coaching, counseling, mentoring, empowering 1 2 3 4 5	representing others, interpreting others' ideas or language 1 2 3 4 5	"signing," miming, acting, singing, or playing an instrument 1 2 3 4 5	consulting, giving advice to groups in your area of expertise 1 2 3 4 5	negotiating between two parties or resolving conflicts 1 2 3 4 5

Look at your list and see which skills are can-do and which are want-to skills. Cross out your can-do skills—that is, any skills you *can* do but don't really *enjoy* using.

Some teens ask if they have to be an expert to keep a particular skill on their list. No, not if you like using the skill and have a moderate amount of experience with it. If a skill shows up in three of your five stories and you like using it, keep it on your list. Remember, it's always possible to develop your skills more fully through education, practice, or concentration.

Now, the really fun part: finding your best skills. Go back to the Skill TIPs list. Of the skills that you like to use and that you used in more than one story, select ten that you most enjoy using. Write each one on a slip of paper or sticky note. Look at each skill. Think about how much you want to use that skill. Do you want to use it often or only occasionally in your work? Place these ten skills in order from your most favorite to your least favorite. This can be hard, but give it a try. When you know your best transferable skills, you have an important clue for finding work you love.

Now, look at the top five: these are your best skills. They are an important part of your parachute. Write these five skills in the My Best Transferable Skills section of the My Parachute diagram (page v). (If you want, use colored pens or pencils to add a little color to your parachute!)

For a quick summary of these steps, see the Identify Your Best Transferable Skills sidebar below.

IDENTIFY YOUR BEST TRANSFERABLE SKILLS

1. Review your list of skills used. Cross out skills you don't enjoy using.
2. Select ten skills you enjoy using.
3. Put the skills in order from most favorite to least favorite.
4. Look at your list of ten skills. The top five are your best transferable skills.
5. Write those skills in the My Best Transferable Skills section of My Parachute (page v).

DISCOVERY EXERCISE

Identify Your Best Self-Management Skills

In your stories, you may have some bits that don't fit into the skill keys, but you think they might be skills. They probably are. You actually have three different kinds of skills.

Transferable skills are also called functional skills. If something functions, it works. When you work, you're using your transferable skills. The five stories you write and check off on the Skill TIPs list help you discover what your favorites are.

Specific knowledge skills are also called work content skills. These skills are what you must *know* in order to do a certain job or activity. In doing most of your interests or hobbies, you have to know skills specific to that activity. For example, in doing her community service project, Serena had to know enough about the sport of downhill skiing that she could show the various techniques to others. Specific knowledge skills can be in interests you already have or ones you want to study further. You already filled these in under My Favorite Interests on the My Parachute diagram (page v). It's always good to remember that your interests involve specific skills that could be useful for your career!

PARACHUTE TIP

You can learn more about self-management skills and their importance to your future career by doing an Internet search. Type the phrase "self management skills" for your search.

Self-management skills are also known as personal traits. These traits describe the unique way you use your skills. Dependable, thorough, energetic, decisive, and compassionate are all self-management skills. For example, one of Serena's traits is that she likes things to be fair. Serena thought the Down

DISCOVERY EXERCISE

To discover your self-management skills, reread your stories. What traits or self-management skills do you see? Write them on sticky notes, then organize them by priority, with your favorite first and so on. Write your top three self-management skills in the My Parachute diagram. As a young worker, you may not have many work content skills or specific kinds of knowledge, but if you are dependable, punctual, and work well with others, you may be able to get hired based on your self-management skills or traits.

syndrome students deserved the opportunity to have fun in the snow. Another trait Serena showed was commitment. Even though the students weren't able to improve as skiers, she didn't stop taking them to the snow.

Whew! You've done a lot of hard work in identifying your favorite interests and your best skills. We hope you had fun too. Maybe you learned something about yourself that you didn't know before—or maybe these exercises confirmed something that you sensed, but weren't certain of, about yourself. Now that you know what you love to do—your interests and the skills you love to use—let's take a look, in the next chapter, at what types of people you like to have around you when you do what you love to do.

IF YOU WANT TO EXPLORE FURTHER . . .

Finding Your Dream Job

Richard N. Bolles, *What Color Is Your Parachute?* 2010 (or latest edition). Ten Speed Press, 2009. Also check out the companion website: **www.JobHuntersBible.com**.

Identifying Your Skills and Planning Your Career

This fun site (the website of European career expert Daniel Porot) will give you lots of information about identifying your skills, planning your career, and searching for jobs. If you want to go right to the skills section, click on the Self-Assessment tab at the bottom left on the home page. **www.careergames.com**

Although the jobs described at California CareerZone are found in California, some may exist in your state too. The website is fun and informative, and it offers several free career assessments. Be sure to use the Reality Check section. It will help you learn what your ideal life may cost. **www.cacareerzone.org**

EUREKA.org provides a comprehensive tool for career and college exploration. At a cost of $30 for an annual subscription, you will be able to explore information on careers, college, financial aid, job search, and starting your own business. **http://eureka.org**

Another site that offers free skills and interest assessments is **www.iseek.org**.

A free skills assessment that links with suggested occupations can be found at **http://online.onet center.org** (click on Skills Search).

Prioritizing: This word means putting items in order of their importance to you. A first priority is what is most important to you. Simple prioritizing can be done by putting each item on a separate sticky note and rearranging them until you have a list that is prioritized. You'll find an online grid and instructions for using one and making custom grids for five to twenty items at the following website (scroll down the far left column for a link to a grid): **www.GroundOfYourOwnChoosing.com**.

2

Who You Love to Work With

YOUR FAVORITE TYPES OF PEOPLE

Have you ever had a part-time or summer job where your work was actually pretty boring but you still liked going to work? If you've had that kind of job, we bet you liked going to work because you enjoyed the people there. Maybe you worked with friends, or perhaps you had a boss who was friendly and helped you learn new skills, or maybe you met interesting people—customers, clients, patients—every day. If you haven't had a part-time or summer job, maybe you've had some of these same experiences in a class. The class itself may have been boring, but you enjoyed going to class because your friends were there, or the teacher cared about you, or class projects took you outside the classroom, where you met interesting people.

Short of being a total hermit, most every job you'll have as a teen or early twentysomething will surround you with people to one degree or another. Later in your career, you may work from a home office or even out of your suitcase and laptop as you travel the world. But as a young person, a good job can be ruined if you're surrounded by difficult people or people you simply aren't comfortable with, and an ordinary, not-so-interesting job can be fun if you work with people you enjoy.

Finding a dream job involves more than discovering what you love to do; it also means discovering what kinds of people you enjoy working with. Let's do that now by going to a "party"!

THE PARTY

Imagine you've received an invitation to a party of people a little older than you. You don't know any of the people well or at all. ("What kind of party is that?!" you ask. Please bear with us, OK?) Below is an aerial view of the room where the party is taking place. For some reason, people with the same or similar interests have all gathered with each other in different corners of the room.

The following is a brief list of the types of people at the party. The terms Realistic, Investigative, Artistic, Social, Enterprising, and Conventional refer to particular types of skills and the people who most enjoy using them. Each category includes a few examples of people who might be in that particular group. In the descriptions of these people, you'll probably notice how their interests and skills work together.

I
INVESTIGATIVE
People who are very curious and like to investigate or analyze things.
Explore it!

R
REALISTIC
People who like nature, athletics, or tools and machinery.
Do it!

A
ARTISTIC
People who are very artistic, imaginative, and innovative.
Invent or create it!

C
CONVENTIONAL
People who like detailed work and like to complete tasks or projects.
Keep it going!

the party

S
SOCIAL
People who like to help, teach, or serve people.
Share it!

E
ENTERPRISING
People who like to start up projects or organizations or influence or persuade people.
Start it or sell it!

Realistic (R): People who like nature, athletics, or tools and machinery. Examples: Tom loves to hike in the mountains and does volunteer trail maintenance. Dee plays on the school soccer team. Paul repairs cars. Louise and Larry build furniture in their father's woodworking shop. Ross grows vegetables for the farmers' market, and Yvette raises dogs to be companion animals for people with disabilities.

Investigative (I): People who are very curious and like to investigate or analyze things. Examples: Jason always wants to know why—why a certain bird is no longer seen in his area, why the brain works the way it does, why one ball team plays better than another. Jessica investigates the best places to take a date—concerts, movies, amusement parks, hiking trails—and writes about them for her school paper. David analyzes everything—from the data in his chemistry experiments to the results of community service projects. Erin, a student council member, wants to figure out why new students have so much difficulty scheduling the classes they need.

Artistic (A): People who are very artistic, imaginative, and innovative. Examples: Ashley draws cartoons. Carlos, Aaron, and Stacy started a band and play at local dances. Daniela designs costumes and sets for school theater productions and is known for being able to create great stuff with few resources. Guy develops his own software for doing computer animation.

Social (S): People who like to help, teach, or serve people. Examples: Isabel, a senior, orients freshmen about life at high school. Steve tutors middle school students in math and English. Keri reads assigned class texts to a blind student. Darin volunteers as a trainer for the school football team, and Bob serves as a peer counselor.

Enterprising (E): People who like to start up projects or organizations, or influence or persuade people. Examples: Dana started a service project where high school students visit the elderly in a convalescent home. Ty, who's running for student body president, persuades people to vote for him. Greg works with kids who are at risk of getting involved with drugs and gangs.

Conventional (C): People who like detailed work and like to complete tasks or projects. Examples: Michael, the treasurer for a service club, keeps detailed financial records of all their fund-raising activities. Kristin works part-time in an insurance office, where she's responsible for keeping all the files up to date. Terri oversees the preparations for the prom, making sure everything that needs to get done gets done.

OK, now you know a little about the kinds of people who'll be at the party. You've just arrived and walk in the front door. (Don't worry about whether you're shy or if you actually have to talk to anyone. That doesn't matter at this party.) Now, we have three questions for you:

1. Which corner of the room would you go to first—that is, which group of people would you most enjoy talking to for the longest time? Write the letter for that corner in the box.

2. After fifteen minutes, everyone else in the corner you chose leaves for another party. Of the groups that still remain, which group would you be drawn to the most? Which people would you most enjoy being with for the longest time? Write the letter for that corner in the box.

3. After fifteen minutes, this group also leaves for another party. You look around and decide where to go next. Of the groups that remain, which one would you most enjoy being with for the longest time? Write the letter for that corner in the box.

The three letters you selected indicate your "Holland Code." The Holland Code is named for Dr. John Holland, a psychologist who did research on "people environments"—that is, the types of people we most like to be with. According to Dr. Holland, everyone has three people environments they prefer from among these six—Realistic, Investigative, Artistic, Social, Enterprising, Conventional. By naming whom you'd prefer to talk with at a party, you've identified your favorite people environment.

(Actually, the Party exercise gives only an approximation of your Holland Code. If you want to take a longer test to more accurately determine your Holland Code, go to www.self-directed-search.com.)

Now, turn to My Parachute (page v) and write your Holland Code in the section entitled My Favorite Types of People. You may also want to write a short sentence or two about these types of people. For example, if your Holland Code is IAS, you might write: "I will enjoy my work most if I am surrounded by people who are very curious and like to investigate or analyze things (I), who are also very innovative and creative (A), and who really want to help or serve people (S)."

Now, look over the traits described for each of the three groups of people you chose and see how much of this is also true of you. We often see ourselves best by looking at others. We call this the Mirror Theory. When we describe the people we would most like to be with, in many cases we have also described ourselves. As the old saying goes, "Birds of a feather flock together." What do you think? Do you see yourself in your favorite types of people?

BOSSES AND CLIENTS

Many young adults find it helpful to describe their idea of a good boss. A good boss can be a great mentor. Teachers are very much like bosses. Some of them make you work very hard, but they manage to pull good work out of you, and you learn a lot from them. When you are just starting out, you want a boss you can learn from. Make a list of characteristics of a good boss for you. Prioritize the list.

If you envision yourself in a job where you have customers, clients, or patients, list what kind of people you'd want them to be. For example, let's say you want to be a speech pathologist working with children and teens. Your patients would be "children and teens." Prioritize this list, as well. Once you've figured out your top two or three descriptors from both prioritized lists, write them into the Favorite Types of People section of your Parachute diagram (or if there's no room, draw a line and write it along the bottom of the page).

Using Career Assessments

You may find that your school offers some written career assessments that you can take as part of a career class or career-center orientation. If your school doesn't have a career program or hasn't offered you any assessments by the time you are fifteen, you can find a few options online (see the next page for resources). Either way, if your school has guidance counselors, show them your results and ask them to help you figure out what the results point to for your future. Not asking for that help can make it hard for you to know how to use the results from the assessments. Keep in mind that assessments have limitations: often they will tell you more about the style with which you perform your skills than what your best skills actually are (which is why filling out your Parachute diagram is so important).

No assessment can give you a final, definitive answer about what job would be perfect for you; it can, however, give you helpful clues as to where you should begin your search for your dream job. In the United States, there are currently about twenty thousand job titles out there for you to choose from. Plus, technology and consumer demand create new jobs every year. Assessments should begin with those twenty thousand, and then narrow the territory down for you. Unfortunately, only a few hundred jobs are included in the databases of career assessments from the get-go. The jobs suggested are those chosen in the past by people who answered the assessment's questions the same way you did. So,

MORE CLUES TO YOUR DREAM JOB

Your Holland Code, the three letters you chose in the Party exercise, not only tells you what type of people you enjoy being with, it also provides clues to jobs you might enjoy. For example, if your three letters are RIA (Realistic, Investigative, Artistic), you may find being a police sketch artist or occupational therapist of interest. If your letters are SEC (Social, Enterprising, Conventional), you might enjoy working as a self-employed wedding planner or an event coordinator.

You can explore job possibilities using your Holland Code at cacareerzone.org, where Holland Codes are given for numerous job descriptions. Although this site is for jobs found in California (there is no national site quite like it), if you come acoss several jobs you like, do your own research to find out whether there are similar jobs where you live—or where you want to live.You can use your three-letter Holland Code to research job possibilities on many websites and in other job-hunting resources. The great thing about this approach is that you may discover interesting jobs you might never have thought of doing, or even jobs you never knew existed.

you'll get a limited list of jobs based on your interests. Still, it's a place to start. Do some research on the Internet or in books like the occupational guides in the library. Learn a bit about each job that's suggested before nixing it. And don't get discouraged if you don't like any of the suggestions you get. Do a little bit of thinking. In what field are the jobs that were suggested for you? Does this field interest you, even if the particular jobs suggested don't? There might be other jobs in this field that would use all your skills. Through research and networking (which we'll explore later in the book), you can find the right job for you.

IF YOU WANT TO EXPLORE FURTHER . . .

The Holland Code

The Party exercise gives an approximation of your Holland Code. If you want to take a longer test to more accurately determine your Holland Code, you can take the Self-Directed Search (SDS), developed by Dr. Holland. The SDS online costs $9.95, and it will take you approximately fifteen minutes to complete. You'll get a personalized report on your computer screen (which you can print out) that lists the occupations and fields of study that most closely match your interests. **www.self-directed-search.com**

If you would like quick, free online assessments (based on Dr. Holland's work) to find jobs you might be interested in, check out **www.cacareerzone.org** and **www.career.missouri.edu/students/ explore/thecareerinterestsgame.php**.

The EUREKA site provides a variety of job-search resources, including job possibilities for various Holland Codes. For a $30 fee, you gain access to all that EUREKA offers. Your school may subscribe to EUREKA and you may also be able to gain free access through a counselor, teacher, or adviser. **http://eureka.org**

Career Assessments

You can learn about the usefulness and limitations of career assessments and find links to online assessments at **www.jobhuntersbible.com/counseling**.

3

—

Where You Love to Be

YOUR IDEAL WORK ENVIRONMENT

Your heart has its own geography, where it prefers to be. That may be by a mountain stream. It may be in the Alps. It may be in the hustle and bustle of the streets of Shanghai or New York. It may be on an Oregon farm. It may be a beach town. Or it might be right where you are now—in your own hometown, in your own backyard, at your high school. Maybe what you'd really love to do is return there someday as a teacher.

Your heart knows the places that it loves. That's what we'll be exploring in this chapter, because finding where you love to be is connected with doing what you love to do and who you want to do it with. It's an important part of being happy with your whole life, not just a small part of it. It's living your whole dream, not just half (or less) of it.

There are lots of ways to consider where you want to be. We'll explore two: your ideal work environment and your ideal community (which includes geographical location). We'll be asking you a lot of questions. You may have answers to some of them and none to others. Maybe you won't even have answers to most of the questions. That's OK. Answer what you can—we're certain you'll have some answers—and just keep the rest of the questions in the back of your mind. Questions, even when you don't know the answer, can help you notice new things or think about things in a way you hadn't thought about them before. For example, if we ask, "Would you rather work outside or indoors?" and you aren't sure, you may start to notice what types of jobs are done indoors or outdoors, or jobs that combine both indoor and outdoor work. Maybe you'd be fine working indoors all the time, but you'd want to live in an area where you could go skiing or surfing on the weekend.

Use the answers you do have as a foundation for further exploration of where you'd love to be—to live, to work, to play. Your answers will change over time, as you visit places you've never been before, as you go to technical school or college, or as you experience your first job. All of these experiences will help you learn what, who, and where is most important in your life.

Each person's ideal working conditions are different. Let's start by exploring something you may never have thought about before: your ideal work environment and what makes it just right for you.

Your Work Environment

When you begin working, roughly one-quarter of your time each week will be at your job. Many a person has gotten what they thought would be their ideal job, only to find that even though they are doing what they most want to do, the workplace is so uncomfortable they must quit. Your work environment needs to be one not only in which you feel comfortable but in which you can thrive. We use the term "environment" here because your ideal "where" includes more than just the location (office, laboratory, farm) where you do your work. The environment also includes, among many other things, your work space (desk, cubicle, lab space, five-hundred-acre ranch, machine shop), physical conditions (windows or no windows, natural or fluorescent lighting, noisy or quiet), atmosphere (formal, casual, amount of contact with people, working style), company size (small, large, local, national, international), and clothing (uniform, suit, jeans).

If you've already had some work experience or if you've visited various workplaces (for example, where your parents work, your doctor's office, your school), think about what you liked or didn't like. Another way to approach this is to think about where you like to study—in a quiet library or in your bedroom with the CD player on, alone or with a group, and so on. Where do you feel

YOUR IDEAL WORK ENVIRONMENT

Answer the following questions as best you can. Because there are a lot of questions, don't try to answer them all at once. Set a timer for ten to fifteen minutes. Answer as many questions as you can during that time. If you're enjoying the exercise when the timer goes off, set it for another ten to fifteen minutes. Another option is to answer some of the questions now, then come back again in a week or two and answer some more. By then, you may have noticed things that you aren't aware of right now. Also, if you think of something not included here, be sure to put that on your list too.

Location

Where would you most like to work . . .

- Indoors or outdoors?
- In an office building? In a machine shop? On a ranch? At your home? Somewhere else?
- In an urban, suburban, or rural area?
- In many locations or one spot (travel or no travel)?

Work Space

What kind of space would you most enjoy . . .

- A cubicle in a large room with lots of other people in their own cubicles?
- Your own desk in a private office?
- Lots of variety—at a desk, in your car, at clients' locations, on airplanes, in hotels?
- A classroom, laboratory, hospital?
- Garage or workshop?
- Outdoors—golf course? ranch? barn? forest? under the sea?
- A place with everything you need—all the latest tools or technology and necessary supplies—or a place where you need to be creative with limited resources, supplies, and equipment?

Physical Conditions

Do you prefer . . .
- Fancy and upscale, moderately nice, or does it not matter?
- Windows that open and close or a climate-controlled building?
- Natural or artificial light?
- A light or dark environment?
- Comfortable temperature or varied temperatures?
- Safe or risky?

Atmosphere

Do you prefer . . .

- Noisy or quiet?
- Calm or bustling?
- Formal or casual—for example, do you want to call your coworkers "Ms. Smith" and "Mr. Jones," or do you prefer that everyone is on a first-name basis?
- Lots of contact with coworkers or very little?
- Lots of contact with the public (clients, patients, customers) or very little?
- Working by yourself with minimal contact with others or working frequently or constantly with others?
- A hierarchical setting (where the boss tells everyone what to do) or a collaborative setting (where the staff works together to determine goals, priorities, and workload)?

Size/Type of Business

Do you prefer . . .

- Large or small? (Think about what "large" and "small" mean to you.)
- Locally owned, national chain, or multinational?
- Knowing all your colleagues and customers or always having a chance to meet someone new?
- A for-profit or nonprofit organization?
- Running your own business?

Clothing

What would you like to wear at work . . .

- A suit?
- Trendy clothes?
- Casual, comfortable clothes?
- Jeans and a casual shirt?
- A uniform (for example, military, firefighter, police officer, waiter/waitress)?
- A lab coat?
- Different clothes for different aspects of your job (for example, a suit when meeting an important client, casual clothes for regular days in the office)?
- Whatever you want to wear?
- Something else?

Write each of your answers on a small slip of paper or sticky note, then put them in order of what is most important to you. (You may want to include one or two items from each of the categories—Location, Work Space, and so on.) Select the five factors that are most important to you. Write these in the My Ideal Work Environment section of My Parachute (page v).

comfortable or uncomfortable? Where would you like to spend more time? The same job (or very similar jobs) can happen in many different environments— some you would love, some you would hate! So let's start exploring what's just right for you.

Your Ideal Community

Everyone has different ideas of what makes a great place to live. If you love to ski, you'll want to be within reasonable distance of the mountains. If you love to surf, you'll want to live near the coast. Another person may want to live near a lake or river, or in the desert. You may want to live near good friends or family. Or, if you have excellent foreign language skills (or want to develop them), you may want to live in a foreign country.

And, more directly related to their jobs, some people want to work within a few blocks of a mass-transit stop. Others want to drive to work and therefore want lots of parking. Some people might want their gym or favorite coffee bar nearby, a grocery store located on the route home from work, or a park close enough for eating lunch or taking a walk. What characteristics do you want in the community where you'll live and work?

YOUR IDEAL COMMUNITY*

Geographical Features

Do you want to live . . .

- In or near the mountains? near the coast? in the desert? on the plains?
- In a small town (less than 5,000 people), a medium-sized city (5,000–20,000), a large city (20,000–500,000), a major metropolitan area (500,000 or larger)?
- In a rural area with a town or city within a reasonable distance or in an isolated area, far from "civilization"?

People

Do you prefer . . .

- A good mix of age, ethnic, economic, and religious groups?
- Mostly people your own age or in your own ethnic, economic, or religious group?
- Living where you already have friends or family or in a place where everyone is new?

Neighborhood/Housing

Do you prefer living . . .

- In a subdivision?
- In an apartment or condominium?
- In a single-family home that doesn't look like everyone else's?

Culture

What is important to you . . .

- Good bookstores, art galleries, libraries, and museums?
- Movie theaters?
- Music, dance, and the arts?
- A local semipro or pro sports team?

Educational Opportunities

What is important to you . . .

- Personal enrichment classes?
- Professional development classes?
- A college or university?

Recreation

What would you like your community to have . . .

- Good parks?
- Bike paths, walking/hiking trails?
- Community sports leagues and facilities?

Commuting

What is important to you . . .

- Commute by car?
- Ability to take mass transit to work?
- Being able to walk or bike to work?

Write the answers to these questions about Your Ideal Community on small slips of paper or sticky notes and put them in order of their importance to you. Then select the top five characteristics and write them in the My Ideal Community section of My Parachute (page v).

* The categories and items on this list are not your only choices. We hope that these suggestions will stimulate additional ideas about what makes a community an ideal one for you. You can also get great ideas by using the categories to brainstorm with a group of friends.

Your Ideal Salary and Level of Responsibility

The last part of your work environment involves determining what level of responsibility you want—both when you first start to work and ultimately—as well as your level of compensation. Your salary level can affect your ideal location, based on what you can afford in what area of the country, and your level of responsibility can affect which people you interact with and in what way.

Because a job finances your life, it's important to know the salary ranges for the different jobs that interest you. There are websites that can help you guesstimate the annual income you need to have for various lifestyles. Salary information is often very general. Career literature usually quotes a national average of the salaries of all people doing that work. To help you make decisions, you'll need to know starting salaries and what more experienced people earn in the parts of the country (or the world) where you most want to live or where there is high demand for the work you want to do.

People generally will tell you how much they paid for something, but most don't like talking about what they earn. Asking people "What's your salary?" or "How much do you earn?" is taboo. If you keep your questions away from their personal earnings, most people you talk with will help you get accurate salary information. You can ask less direct questions, such as, "The average starting salary nationally is $41,750 a year. Are local starting salaries similar?" or "I've read that the average annual salary for an experienced worker is about $63,000. What is the salary range for an experienced worker in this area?" Starting and average wages for lots of occupations can be found online (see sidebar). If you are interested in jobs that involve sales, this type of work usually pays a base salary plus commissions. You need to know that starting base salary so you can figure out if you could survive on the base salary, given your debts and monthly expenses.

The force that drives salaries up or down is supply and demand. If there is a great supply of workers with certain skills, but little demand for workers with those skills, the salary for that work will be low. Salaries rise when there aren't enough workers (supply) to meet the demand. The ideal situation is to find jobs that you like a lot and that are in high demand. If you can't find both

HELPFUL SITES FOR SALARY INFO

www.collegegrad.com
www.eureka.org
www.salary.com (note that this site charges a fee for reports beyond basic information)

in the same kind of work, you'll have to figure out whether it's more important to you to have a steady income or work in a field that absolutely fascinates you but may not pay so well.

YOUR IDEAL SALARY AND LEVEL OF RESPONSIBILITY

Some people want to earn as much money as they can. Others want to earn enough to take care of themselves, but still have time for hobbies and friends. Ask yourself,

"What salary do I want to make when I get out of school?"

"What salary do I hope to be making after five years of experience?"

"What do I want my top salary to be?"

"What jobs that interest me pay what I hope to earn?"

You can learn about salaries for jobs by reading job descriptions at career information sites like **online.onetcenter.org** or **cacareerzone.org**. Find people doing these jobs and confirm the starting or average salaries in your area or where you'd like to live. Then figure out your ideal salary, which is the amount it will take to finance your preferred lifestyle. If you don't know what your preferred lifestyle might cost, websites like **www.californiarealitycheck.com** and **www.jumpstartcoalition.org/realitycheck** can help you figure it out. Write your likely starting salary and your ideal salary on your Parachute diagram in the section labeled Salary. This is your salary range.

Finally, let's think about what level of responsibility appeals most to you. Do you want to be an employee, salesperson, supervisor, or manager—or do you want to own the place? Some people might call this the job's "level of worry." If you don't want the worries of work to follow you home, choose your level carefully. And if you manage your career well, although you may start out at one point—say, entry level—over time you can gain the education and experience you need to advance. Briefly summarize what level of responsibility you want and write that on your Parachute diagram.

IF YOU WANT TO EXPLORE FURTHER . . .

Work Environment

If you're interested in learning more about the working conditions for particular jobs, check out the Occupational Outlook Handbook, which can be found at this website: **www.bls.gov/oco/home.htm**.

This website has free resources and a survey to help you identify your ideal workplace: **www.theworkplacereview.com/Detective_Guidebook.php**.

Geographical Location or Community

Want to investigate places that you'd like to live? Visit these websites:

www.bestplaces.net/fybp

www.findutopia.com

www.findyourspot.com

If you'd like to live abroad, see Elizabeth Kruempelmann's *The Global Citizen: A Guide to Creating an International Life and Career* (Ten Speed Press, 2004). In some fields, international experience may qualify you for a higher starting salary.

Interested in checking out various geographical locations with short-term jobs? See Michael Landes's *The Back Door Guide to Short-Term Job Adventures*, 4th ed. (Ten Speed Press, 2005).

Volunteer work is another way to learn about different places. The following books will help you learn more about international volunteer opportunities:

Bill McMillon, *Volunteer Vacations: Short-Term Adventures That Will Benefit You and Others*, revised 10th ed. (Chicago Review Press, 2009)

Joseph Collins, *How to Live Your Dream of Volunteering Overseas* (Penguin, 2001)

Charlotte Hindel et. al., *Volunteer: A Traveler's Guide to Making a Difference around the World* (Lonely Planet, 2007)

If part of your life's dream includes working your way around the world, plan your adventure using a book like Susan Griffith's *Work Your Way around the World*, 13th ed. (Crimson Pubishing, 2008).

4

Putting the Pieces Together

IDENTIFYING YOUR POTENTIAL DREAM JOBS

Are you ready for the next step? In this chapter you'll finish filling out the My Parachute diagram (page v) and begin to identify your potential dream jobs. All the hard work you did in the previous three chapters has produced the pieces of your career puzzle. As you begin to identify potential dream jobs (or fields in which you are likely to find your dream job), you'll begin to see the pieces come together to form new possibilities and directions for further exploration.

Though it can be tempting, we encourage you not to narrow your options for your dream job too quickly—that is, don't lock yourself into a particular job title without looking at all the possibilities. In general, we humans are more comfortable with labels than lists. It's certainly easier to talk about job titles than to give someone a list of skills that you like and want to use. But if you focus on a job title too soon, before investigating several jobs that might use similar skills, you may not learn about work that could be a better match for your best skills and favorite interests—in other words, you just might pass your dream job by.

If you didn't have your parachute, the process of finding your dream job would be much harder. As you know, it's very hard to find something when you don't know what you're looking for! That's why your parachute is so important. The information that you've gathered on page v will help you recognize your dream job when you come across it.

Finding Your Field of Interest

A good job for you will use most of your favorite interests and skills. Turn to My Parachute (page v) and take a look at My Favorite Interests. What did you write there? Sometimes the process of finding your dream job, or potential dream job, involves a little "translation"—by which we mean taking your favorite interests and determining the occupational field in which they fit. Sometimes the fields are much broader or much more numerous than you realize at first.

> I wish I would have known that there were opportunities to earn a comfortable living much closer to the types of dreams and interests that I had in high school. I was an avid lover of maps back then. Had I known that being a cartographer was an available career, I would have fervently pursued it.
>
> —ADAM HOVERMAN, DO, family practice physician, age 30

If one of your interests is skateboarding, your fields might be athletics, recreation, or kinesiology (the study of the principles of mechanics and anatomy in relation to human movement). If you choose the field of athletics, you might become a skateboarding coach; if recreation, you might become involved with designing a skateboard park or program for skateboarders; if kinesiology, you might design skateboards that are easier and safer to use, and also more flexible for doing various maneuvers. In each case, your training and education (for example, choice of training or college majors) would vary.

Here's another example. One of Tamara's interests is medicine. Because her best skills involve taking care of sick or injured people, she wants to be a nurse. But there are many types of nurses and many places in which Tamara can use her nursing skills. What kind of nurse she becomes will depend on what type of training she completes, what major she chooses, and also what her other interests are. The field of medicine is quite broad. Here are some nursing jobs Tamara could pursue:

- If she wants to work with children, she could be a pediatric nurse. Pediatrics is the field in which she'd use her nursing skills.

- If cancer care is a strong interest, she could be an oncology nurse. (Field = oncology)

- If she is most interested in emergency medicine, she could be an emergency room nurse, work on a search-and-rescue team, or be part of a Life Flight medical team. (Field = emergency medicine)

- If Tamara is also very interested in recreation, she could be a nurse on a cruise ship or at a large resort. (Field = recreation)

As you can see in Tamara's case, and in the case of someone who likes skateboarding, the same job can happen in many different fields, some of which you'd like and some you'd hate!

FINDING YOUR FIELDS OF INTEREST

1. Turn to My Parachute (page v) and look at the section entitled My Favorite Interests.
2. Consider each of one your interests. What are the different occupational fields where could you use your interests? Try to name at least two or three for each interest.
3. List these jobs on a separate piece of paper or in your journal. This list isn't set in stone; as you learn more about different jobs you may want to cross out some items or add new ones.

If you need some help translating your favorite interests into particular jobs or careers, talk with your parents, school counselor, or librarian, or the staff person at a career center. Many websites, like **www.bls.gov/k12**, can also help to translate your interests into fields or industries.

DISCOVERY EXERCISE

Exploring Potential Dream Jobs

Now that you've identified your fields of interest, it's time to explore some potential dream jobs. Perhaps you have a clear idea of what those jobs may be. If so, that's great. But if you don't, don't despair. Here are some steps you can take to help you discover potential dream jobs to explore:

- Show your parachute to people whose opinions and suggestions you trust. Ask them for ideas about jobs that might match your fields of interest and your skills.

- Read tons of information about different occupations. Libraries and career centers have materials about many kinds of work. Start by finding and reading this general information. Ask the librarian or career center staff to direct you to resources that will help you find jobs that fit your fields of interest and skills.

- Do an Internet search to find information about specific jobs or careers. (There's a list of useful websites at the end of this chapter.)

- Read magazines and newspapers and watch TV. When jobs are mentioned, which jobs interest you? Keep a list of those jobs or cut out articles on them.

- One of the best ways to figure out if a line of work is a good match for you is to talk to people who have worked in that field for a while. If you want to continue living in the same region where you currently live, there are several ways to find local people doing work that interests you:

  - Ask adults you know if they know people who work in the fields that interest you or do some of the jobs that interest you. Get contact information (name, email, phone number, or mailing address) for each name you get. Have an adult you trust help you come up with a phone script or email asking for time to talk with them about their jobs or career.

  - Check out the Yellow Pages of your local phone book. Start with Z and read backward (starting at the back puts the information in an unexpected order, so you see things you'd miss if you started with A as usual). The Yellow Pages list many of the jobs that exist where you live. Make a list of categories that have jobs you are curious about. Call the businesses listed in these categories to find someone to talk with about the jobs that interest you most. (City, county, state, and federal government agencies have jobs too. These agencies are generally listed in the front of phone books.)

  - Find the labor force projections for the county in which you live. Contact your local state employment office (every county has at least one location). These projections let you see which occupations are in greatest demand where you live (or want to live). Not all projections become reality—another reason to talk with people in your area who are doing jobs you might like or to employers who hire for those jobs. To make a good decision about what careers to pursue, you need firsthand information. Ask your favorite adults to help you find people to interview. And remember, this is just to broaden your information gathering—such projections shouldn't be the basis for a life decision, as they can and do change.

After you've gone through these steps, you should have at least two or three job possibilities to explore.

REALITY CHECK

Thirty-eight percent of the college graduates we surveyed said that their knowledge of the work world was extremely limited. They felt they had not chosen the best major and would have made very different career choices if they had known about a greater variety of jobs. Due to student loans and other financial realities, going back to school for further studies wouldn't be possible until they had worked a few years,

In contrast, a study of university graduates in England reported only 20 percent felt they had studied the wrong subject. The difference? University-bound students in Great Britain have an extra year of high school and must take a "gap year" before continuing to higher education. British students start college older (in their early twenties) and are encouraged to use their gap year to explore the field in which they hope to work.

Two New Research Tools:
Networking and Information Interviews

Once you've gathered and read a lot of written information about potential dream jobs, your next step is to explore these jobs further by talking with people who actually do the work that interests you. Having filled in your Parachute diagram and read about a few dozen jobs, you should now be able to name three different fields or jobs that might match your parachute. By talking with people in the fields that interest you or to people doing the same job you want, you get a more accurate picture of what the work entails, especially if you meet with your interview subject at the worksite.

In career exploration and job-search classes, this informal research goes by many names. You'll hear it called networking, field research, doing information interviews, and other phrases. Essentially, it's just gathering information you need by talking to people.

Networking

The older you get, the more you'll hear the word "networking." Networking is about using connections to reach your goals. It is a big part of today's job-search and career strategies. Your choices of jobs, colleges, courses to take, and skills to learn will all be influenced by the way you network. Whether you want to find a new veterinarian, a new dance club, or a new job, networking can help.

Networking can be done formally or informally.

Informal networking happens when you are trying to uncover a resource or learn more about an issue, hobby, or activity. If you've ever asked someone where they bought their cool shoes or tried to find an extra ticket to a must-see concert, you've done informal networking.

For example, Jesse likes to build and fly remote-control model planes. He's got a summer job working at a residential camp for eight weeks that's several hours away from where he lives. Jesse is going to take a couple of planes with him so he can fly them when he's not working. He wants to find other people in the area who fly model planes. How can he do that?

If Jesse belongs to a club, he can ask members if they know of a club near the camp or anyone in that area who flies model planes. He could also see if there's a hobby store in the town nearest the camp and ask there about a club or if there is a local airstrip for remote-control planes. Jesse might find helpful information on the Internet or in a magazine dedicated to the sport. From such articles, Jesse might find a club near his work or the names of people he can contact for more information about where to fly his planes.

Formal networking is more focused. Information interviewing is an example of formal networking. Your focus is to gather information about current conditions and trends in specific fields or jobs.

Whether you contact people through the Internet or face-to-face, getting good career information or getting a job is still a people-to-people activity. You will find more job opportunities through formal networking than you ever will through the want ads. Through networking you can also find

- What the work environment is like and whether it suits you.

- The jargon, trends, and issues of the field.

- Mentors and leaders in the field or industry that interests you.

- Ideas for better or faster ways to get job qualifications.

Networking is a skill you want to get good at, because you'll need to use it throughout your life.

Information Interviews

Your parents, relatives, parents of your friends, teachers, or other adults can help you find people who have jobs you're curious about. You can also find people to talk with through the local Yellow Pages and the Internet, or by sending out a request through Facebook, MySpace, or any other social networking site to which you belong. Talk to at least three people with a particular job or career before you decide whether to toss it out or pursue it as a goal. Each person's experience with and feelings about the job will vary. Try to gather the most accurate information about the job that you can. By talking with more than one person, you're likely to get a more balanced view of a job.

You can do some of these interviews over the phone. It's even better, though, to interview people at their worksites so you can see the work environment. (How does it compare to your ideal work environment, which you listed on your parachute?) Until you see the actual work setting for particular jobs, you won't have a complete picture of what doing each job will really be like. And here's a safety tip: never go alone to an information interview if you

PRACTICE INFORMATION INTERVIEWING

If you're shy or haven't had much experience talking to people about their work, build your skills by doing practice interviews. Before you begin interviewing people about jobs that interest you, talk with people doing jobs that you're curious about but don't necessarily want to do yourself. Or talk with people doing jobs that relate to your hobbies or interests—topics you know something about and really like to talk about. If you do two to five practice interviews, you'll learn what it feels like to have a conversation about a mutual interest. Talking about something you enjoy isn't scary or intimidating at all! By doing practice interviews, you can learn how to gather information about jobs without having to worry about the possibility that someday you'll be working with or for this person.

are meeting a stranger (even though someone you trust made the recommendation). If you are not doing your interview over the phone or email, always meet at a worksite when other people are around.

Setting Up Information Interviews

WHO DO I TALK TO?

Speak with a worker actually doing the job that interests you. This person's boss may be easier to find, and you may need to talk with the boss to get connected with someone who does the job you want information about. But don't stop with the person in charge. You need to know what it's like to do the job from an employee perspective.

WILL I NEED AN APPOINTMENT?

Often you will. If the jobs that interest you are in retail stores or fairly public businesses or places, you may be able to walk in at a slow time and find someone who will talk with you. "What's it like to work here?" is an easy way to get someone talking.

But if the job or organization you want to learn more about is far away or limits public access, or if the person doing the work is very busy, you'll need to make an appointment for a fifteen-minute conversation. You can make the appointment by phone.

WHAT DO I SAY TO MAKE AN APPOINTMENT?

Develop a "pitch." Write a short script to introduce yourself to the person you'd like to interview. Here's a sample:

Hi, my name is Megan. My father gave me your name because you own a mobile pet-care business. I like animals very much, and I'd like to learn more about businesses that involve pets. Could I make an appointment to talk with you about your work? I wouldn't need more than fifteen minutes of your time.

People may want to know more about you, so be ready to add information about who you are and why you want to talk with them.

WHAT IF I FREEZE ON THE PHONE WHILE MAKING AN APPOINTMENT?

Have your script written out and in front of you when you call. If you experience a brain freeze, quickly refer to your script.

CAN I FIRST CONTACT SOMEONE WITH A NOTE?

If you don't like the idea of calling someone you don't know who doesn't know you (in the sales field, this practice is known as "cold calling"), you can send them a note—through either the U.S. mail or email. Obviously, you will need to know their mailing or email address. The Internet and adults you know can help you learn this information. Mention in your email that you will follow up with a phone call to set up an appointment—and be sure to make that follow-up call. Here is a sample of a written request:

Dear Amanda Ruiz:

My name is Taneesha Jones. I am currently studying mechanical engineering and robotics at Tidewater Community College. My robotics teacher showed me an article on bionic limbs that you had written for LiveSience.com. My ultimate career goal is to assist in creating new medical equipment that will help people regain their mobility after spinal injuries. I would like to work for a year or two before transferring to a university.

I know you must be very busy, but I am hoping you can spare twenty minutes to talk with me about your career. I would also like your suggestions as to what entry-level jobs I might qualify for and what college major might best prepare me for future jobs.

If you would reply with some convenient times that I might phone you to set up an appointment, I would be very grateful.

Sincerely, Taneesha Jones

WILL SOMEONE ACTUALLY SEE ME?

Yes. Not everyone will say yes, of course, but if you speak courteously when requesting an appointment, communicate clearly what you want from them, and show gratitude for their time, about eight out of ten people will talk to you.

In general, people love to talk about themselves. Also, most of them remember being in high school and not having a clue about how to get a job. Many of those who do talk with you will be very impressed that you're doing research to learn about jobs that will be a good fit for you. Those who are impressed will be very helpful.

And if they like what they do, you'll probably have to work hard to keep the conversation on track so you can ask all your questions in just fifteen minutes! To keep your interviewees on track, tell them at the beginning of your interview that you have five or six questions. To keep your appointment within fifteen to twenty minutes, they'll have just two minutes per question. If they want, they can invite you to stay a bit longer.

When you go for the interview, be sure to show up on time and be organized. Have your questions ready, and come prepared to take notes about their answers.

WHY WILL BUSY ADULTS AGREE TO MEET WITH ME?

As a student researching your career goals, you've got the Wow factor. Adults know that it may take working at several jobs before you find the best fit, and they will be impressed that you are doing this kind of research to find your first career path. Don't be surprised if some of those you interview say things like, "Wow, I'm so impressed you are taking the time to find a good job fit" or "Wow, I wish I had done this kind of career investigation when I was your age."

DO I HAVE TO GO ALONE?

No. You can have one of your parents, grandparents, or another adult go with you until you feel comfortable on your own. You can also take a friend with you. Be sure to choose one who knows how to behave in business situations and won't embarrass you. If you want someone to go with you, though, it's good business etiquette to ask the person you're interviewing whether that's OK. Don't just show up with another person.

WHAT SHOULD I ASK THE PERSON I'M INTERVIEWING?

You may have specific questions you want to ask, or questions may arise during the interview. That's great, but be sure you ask the following five questions, which will give you a good sense of what the job is really like and how you can get a job like this:

1. How did you get into your job? What kind of training or education did you have?

2. What three to five tasks do you do most often? How often? What skills are necessary to do these tasks?

3. What do you like about your job? What don't you like about your job?

4. What do you see happening in your field of work in the next five to ten years?

5. Do you know someone else doing this (or similar) work with whom I could talk?

As you listen to the person's answers, take notes. (You can do this when you read about jobs too.) Divide the information into the same categories as those on My Parachute (page v). For example, if you're interviewing Dr. Kelly, a veterinarian, you may start by asking her, "How did you get into your job?" She may answer, "Well, I've loved animals since I was a little kid. I always had cats, dogs, birds, horses, and all kinds of other pets. Whenever one of them got hurt, I'd calm them down, clean out the wound—if it wasn't too serious—and help them heal. I always thought it would be great to be able to help animals all the time when I grew up, so I became a veterinarian."

In her answer, Dr. Kelly told you about her interest in animals and the skills she had working with them. So in Dr. Kelly's parachute, under *My Favorite Interests*, you would write "caring for animals" and under *My Best Transferable Skills*, you'd write "calming animals and cleaning their wounds."

Later in your interview, Dr. Kelly may mention that it's important for her to work with people who are compassionate and who love animals (*My Favorite Types of People*). She may also say that she chose to become a large-animal veterinarian, working mainly with horses, cattle, and sheep, because she loves to work outside (*My Ideal Work Environment*) and live in a rural area where people—ranchers, cowhands, farmers—work with animals for a living (*My Ideal Community*).

Having the information in the same categories as your own parachute will make it easier for you to compare the interviewee's parachute with yours. This way of organizing the information you get about various jobs allows you to see where your parachute and theirs are the same and where they're different.

One of the most important questions you can ask the people you interview is the last one: "Do you know someone else doing this (or similar) work with whom I could talk?" Dr. Kelly, for instance, might give you the name of a small-animal veterinarian, a zoo or racetrack veterinarian, and a veterinary technician. By asking for names of other people to talk with, you create additional contacts. If you get two or three names from each person you talk to, you'll soon have a huge resource for learning about jobs you might like. You'll also be making contacts that may be useful later on in your job search.

Of course, it makes no sense to follow up and interview additional people when it's clear that you really aren't interested in what they do. For example, you might decide, after interviewing Dr. Kelly and another veterinarian, that you really don't want to have to go through all the years of school and all those science classes to work with animals. But the idea of being a veterinary technician is very appealing, so you could then interview two or three more vet techs.

Once you know that a particular career or type of work doesn't match your parachute, or overlaps only a little bit, how do you find people whose work may suit you better? The Job Meter can help you formulate questions that will lead you to jobs that better match your parachute.

Using the Job Meter

The Job Meter, which is the creation of Marty Nemko, PhD, helps you find people whose work is closer to what you want to do. (You can find more of Dr. Nemko's brilliant ideas at www.martynemko.com.) Here's how to use the Job Meter:

1. As you think about a job or listen to someone describe theirs, give the job a rating on a scale of 1 to 10 (1 = awful; 10 = perfect).

2. If you rate the job less than 9, ask yourself, "What would have to be different about this job in order for it to be a 10?"

3. If you're in an information interview, describe how the job of your dreams differs from the job of the person you're talking with. Try to do so without sounding rude; for example, don't say, "Your job sounds really awful!" Ask if the interviewee knows someone whose job is more like what you're looking for.

A SAMPLE JOB METER

Eric is seventeen. Last week he did an information interview with Steve, a stockbroker. Eric gave that job a rank of 3 on his Job Meter. It did involve math, analysis of information, and using numbers as a reasoning tool—some of Eric's best skills. But Steve worked in a high-rise building downtown, the work environment was very formal, and his colleagues—who looked stressed-out—worked in little offices. None of this appealed to Eric.

Today Eric is meeting with his mom's cousin Leah. She's barely thirty and has her own small business as a certified public accountant (CPA). She works in an old house that's been converted into office suites. The surrounding neighborhood has big, leafy trees and a couple of outdoor cafés. Leah's workplace feels much more comfortable to Eric than the stockbroker's office. After listening to Leah describe what she does, Eric decides to tell her about the Job Meter, an idea a teacher had explained in a career-planning class. He asks Leah what rating she'd give her job.

"A 9.9," she flashed back at him. "What do you think of it?"

Eric hesitated, then answered, "Maybe a 5 or 6. My teacher said that a job needs to be at least an 8 to be a good career target."

Luckily Leah wasn't insulted. She smiled and asked, "What would have to be different about the job for it to be a 9 or 10 for you?"

"I'm not sure I want to have my own business or lots of people as clients. I think I'd like to use my math to gather information and write reports that would go to a boss or one client. And both you and Steve, the stockbroker I interviewed last week, spend a lot of time meeting new people. I guess that's to expand your business?"

"Yes. I belong to a service club, a community business group, and a women's professional organization. I review the annual taxes for the preschool my son goes to, and I've volunteered to be the treasurer for the co-op kindergarten he'll attend next year. I'd like to think I'm more subtle than wearing a button that says, 'I'm a CPA and I need your business,' but I'm constantly looking for ways to meet people who may need my services."

"I don't think I'd like that part, constantly meeting new people. I'd also like my day to be split between working inside and outdoors."

Leah thought for a while, then said, "I've got clients who do all kinds of different jobs. Give me a week to go through my files. I also need to check with them to ask if I can give you their names. I'll find some more people for you to talk with about careers that use math."

"Thanks, Leah. I appreciate your help," Eric responded. "The more people I talk with, the more likely it is that I'll find a job that's a good fit for me."

Some people can rate a job, evaluate it, and describe how their dream job differs as they interview someone. Others need time to think over what they've heard. If you're the second type, you can call people back. Give them a description of the skills, activities, fields of interest, or working conditions that would make a job a 10 for you. To give the person you interviewed time to think of some good people for you to talk to, you could also include this information in your thank-you note (see below) and tell them you'll call to ask for their suggestions.

Writing a Thank-You Note

After each information interview, always send a thank-you note. Why? Whenever you meet with people or interview them on the phone or by email, they give you something very valuable—their time, experience, and wisdom. Any gift of value deserves to be acknowledged. The people you interview will appreciate that you recognize the value of their time and life experience. They'll be impressed too, and most likely will be more inclined to help you again if you should need additional information in the future.

During an interview, be sure to get a business card. For interviewees who don't have one, ask for their job title, the correct spelling of their name, and the name of the company they work for. Getting this information correct shows that you've taken the interview seriously and appreciate the help the person has given you.

Here are some tips on how to write a thank-you note:

- Buy some plain thank-you notes (drugstores and stationery stores carry them) and some stamps.

- Unless your handwriting is very good, type your thank-you note and print it out. You can glue your note inside a card or create a card online to print out. No cutesy Hello Kitty or far-out images. You are writing a note to a businessperson, not a friend.

- Keep it simple. A thank-you note can be just two or three sentences.

- Write and send your note within twenty-four hours after your appointment. A thank-you note that arrives a week later seems like an afterthought, not gratitude.

Here's an example:

Dear Mr./Ms./Dr. _____ :

Thank you for talking with me yesterday about your work. The information you gave me was quite helpful. I very much appreciate that you were willing to take the time to meet with me.

If I decide to become a _____ , I will probably have more questions for you.

Sincerely,
Your Name

If the person you met with said something particularly helpful, gave you a good suggestion, or recommended another contact who's already agreed to meet with you, you may want to mention those things in your note. You can ask for suggestions about jobs that might earn a 10 on your Job Meter. For example, if you crave a job with an international focus, ask your interviewee whether he or she knows of organizations or jobs that have that element.

You can email a thank-you note too. Email is immediate and easy to read. Be sure to follow these guidelines:

- Use standard English (don't write in all caps or all lowercase).

- Use proper punctuation and grammar (no run-on or stream-of-consciousness type sentences).

- When you're finished, run the spell-check tool in your email program.

- Ask an adult to proofread the note; spell-check is helpful but not foolproof!

After Your Information Interviews

When you've completed your information interviews, you should have a much clearer idea of your potential dream jobs. Write down the three that you like the most and keep learning about them.

All of your hard work will not only help you find your dream job, but may also help you in more immediate ways. You can use everything you've written on your parachute—what you've learned about yourself and what you've learned from information interviews—to approach many situations with a new

WHAT IF MY DREAM JOB IS WORKING FOR MYSELF?

If you talk with ten or more people who are doing the kind of work you want to do, and you think, "I'd rather start my own business," you aren't alone. There are more entrepreneurs in the Millennial Generation than in any previous generation. You may like to tinker, have an idea for how to make something better, or want provide a service that you see a need for. People who set up their own businesses for profit are called "entrepreneurs." People who establish a nonprofit to provide services to a special population or about a special issue are called "social entrepreneurs."

Whichever title appeals to you, you can find related articles, blogs, associations, summer camps, competitions, and success stories on the Internet and in books. While you are living at home is a great time to create your own business, because your parents are taking care of your personal overhead. If you can find an inexpensive way to create and market a product or service (like the eleven- and nine-year-old brothers who created a math game sold for iPhones), you can be one step closer to your dream job—and your dream life.

sense of focus and direction. Starting to learn what your dream job is will help you find more satisfying summer jobs, internships, or part-time work, and it may just help you choose a college major.

Wow! You've done a lot of good work discovering what you love to do, who your favorite types of people are, and where you'd like to work and live. Maybe some questions still need answering, but that's fine. Those answers will come with time. We hope you've discovered some things about yourself that you didn't even know and confirmed some things you did know.

The discoveries you've made about yourself in part 1 lay the foundation for the practical steps you can take to land your dream job, presented in part 3. But first, in part 2 we want to take a look at getting the most out of high school and college (if you plan to go to college), as well as some other tools that can get you further down the road toward finding your dream job.

IF YOU WANT TO EXPLORE FURTHER . . .

Finding Potential Dream Jobs

The Occupational Information Network (O*Net Online) has full descriptions of hundreds of occupations: **http://online.onetcenter.org**.

For an alphabetical list of jobs with comprehensive information, including salary and training requirements, check out this website: **http://stats.bls.gov/oco**.

For stories of young adults who have found their dream jobs through community college programs, go to **www.whodouwant2b.com**.

Junior Achievement offers useful career information at **http://studentcenter.ja.org/careers/Pages/default.aspx**.

Your reaction to the video at this link will help you determine whether you want to work to live or live to work: **www.youtube.com/watch?v=k7JII959sIY**.

Apprenticeships, Internships, Study Abroad, and Other Opportunities

The U.S. Department of Labor can provide information on different kinds of work and apprenticeships. There are over twenty-nine thousand different apprenticeship programs offered by the Department of Labor. Formal apprenticeships are unique in that you're paid to work while you learn. You must attend training classes as well. Check out this website: **www.careervoyages.gov**.

For listings of internships, apprenticeships, volunteer, and study-abroad opportunities, check out this website: **http://rileyguide.com/intern.html**.

Economics

Keynes, John. *The General Theory of Employment, Interest and Money*. Signalman Publishing, 2009.

Kiosaka, Robert. *Rich Dad, Poor Dad for Teens: The Secrets about Money—That You Don't Learn in School!* Running Press Miniature Editions, 2009.

Smith, Adam. *Wealth of Nations*. Prometheus Books, 1991.

If you want to learn more about the American system of money, this forty-seven-minute animated video covers the basics: **www.filmsforaction.org/film/?Film=247&Title=Money_As_Debt**.

John Gerzema, Chief Insights Officer (I want this job title!) at Young & Rubican explains how the consumer economy may recover: **www.youtube.com/watch?v=ONXYcN-7k1Y**.

General Job-Hunting and Career Information

For the inside scoop, see Michael Gregory's *The Career Chronicles: An Insider's Guide to What Jobs Are Really Like—the Good, the Bad, and the Ugly from over 750 Professionals* (New World Library, 2008).

Use this link for a list of a hundred career-related blogs that cover an amazing variety of topics: **www.careerrocketeer.com/2009/07/100-career-blogs-all-professionals-must.html#comments**.

This informative Canadian site has great general information about jobs and career planning: **http://nextsteps.org**.

Through RoadTripNation, young adults have interviewed working people on six continents. Their goal: to make sure every individual has the opportunity to find his or her own road in life. Listen to interviews with fascinating people at **www.roadtripnation.com**.

For creative ideas to help you build your first career path, see the website of Marty Nemko, PhD (creator of the Job Meter). Click on "Find a Career" in the upper left under *Article Topics*: **www.martynemko.com**.

Websites for Young Entrepreneurs

www.sba.gov/teens

www.score.org/young.html

Junior Achievement operates programs in most U.S. states and many European countries: **http://studentcenter.ja.org/aspx/PlanBusiness/**.

Do You Need a Career Coach?

Career coaching can help high school students broaden their horizons about the type of major they might pursue in college or the type of career they might launch into after high school. A coach can help you better discover your marketable skills, identify your fields of fascination, and determine viable options to pursue once you have obtained your high school degree. A coach will carefully listen to your wants, needs, and goals; during the coaching sessions the coach uses questions, written exercises, and feedback to help you consider options and make informed decisions. To learn more about what a career coach can do for you, visit **www.youthleadershipcareers.com**.

Excellent career coaching can also be found at **www.jobfindingpartners.com**.

PART TWO

ON THE WAY TO YOUR FUTURE

High school students need encouragement to seek out careers that build on what they love to do already. So often salary, prestige, or ambition gets in the way of chasing after the golden key to what already motivates and inspires. Feel the freedom to go in the direction that your dreams move, however and wherever that freedom is found.

—ADAM HOVERMAN, DO, family practice physician, age 30

DOES it sometimes seem that the future is very far away? Does it seem that doing what you love to do is just a fantasy? If you do nothing now—if you just hope that this will somehow increase your options—you are likely to graduate and have no idea how to turn your career fantasies into a real job. But there are steps you can take to help that fantasy become reality, because right now, at this very moment, you are creating your future. In this part of the book, we'll look at some of the steps you can take to realize the future you want.

In chapter 5, you'll discover ways to make the most of your high school years and use them to move yourself closer to finding and enjoying your dream job. Chapter 6 will tell you how you can use those college years most productively to prepare yourself for work you'll love—and it's not only for those of you who plan to go to college. Chapter 6 actually includes a lot of great information and advice about higher education for everyone. In chapter 7 you'll learn to set goals—a tool that will help you not only to shape your future but also to get through this school year! Finally, chapter 8 gives you a new spin on an old tool: using social networking sites for career exploration and job search.

This exploration—making the most of high school and college and learning new tools—will give you the freedom to follow your dreams and move confidently into the future and toward finding work that you'll love.

5
—
What Do I Do Now?

MAKING THE MOST OF HIGH SCHOOL

High school matters! And not as a boring waiting room until graduation or college, when "real life" begins. You can use your high school years to learn technical skills, put together academic and activity achievements to help you get into college, explore careers, and put together a detailed plan. Students usually know that to succeed they need reasonably good grades. What most don't know is the importance of making tentative career decisions and creating a plan for how to achieve career and life goals.

Why do you need a detailed plan? Studies of students—whether they go to college or not—show that those who achieve their life and career ambitions have a detailed plan. The plan gives them focus. They know why they are in school and how their classes relate to their plan. They also know obstacles that are likely to come up and have created strategies for overcoming those obstacles.

Does getting a job or starting a career seem light-years away? For some of you, that may almost be true. (We say "almost" because the future actually seems to come more quickly than we expect!) Transitioning from high school to your preferred career or a full-time job you enjoy can take up to ten years.

This is one reason you want to start work on this transition while you are still in high school. You can use your high school classes and extracurricular activities to build a strong foundation for your first career pathway.

Just like a savvy politician, you can use your time in high school to set up a "campaign" that will help you achieve your future career goals. This campaign includes increasing your awareness of the work world, developing job-search skills, creating a career portfolio, and considering whether you want or need to go to college. We'll explore all of those things in this chapter. And because it's good to think about what lies ahead, we'll also take a brief look at what comes after high school.

Awareness of the Work World

As you learn more about the world of work, your awareness of career possibilities and different kinds of jobs grows. All the work you've done in the preceding chapters—exploring your interests, skills, and preferences concerning work environments and people to work with, and identifying potential dream jobs—provides a solid foundation for your growing awareness.

Even without realizing it, you're probably already doing things that are helping your awareness to grow. You may, for example, be paying more attention to what people do to earn a living. You may take a career interest assessment that suggests some jobs you might like but didn't know about previously. You may have older friends or siblings who have left school and started jobs that you didn't even know existed. You may notice who enjoys their work, and who doesn't.

You can also help your awareness of the work world grow by focusing some of your high school experiences—class assignments, extracurricular activities, part-time or summer work—on possibilities for your future. Let's take a brief look at some of your options.

Class Assignments

Need to do a book report? Read a book about a superstar in the industry that most interests you. Or pick one of the many helpful books listed at the end of this chapter. Need to do a report? Pick a profession, field, or industry that interests you and do a research paper. You might, for example, research which Fortune 500 companies were started by people who didn't finish college. Need to do a presentation? Report on what you learned in preparing your parachute and conducting your information interviews. In doing a presentation like this, you not only fulfill a class requirement, but you may also help your friends and classmates learn good skills for finding work they'll love.

If your school has a community service requirement for graduation, look for ways in which you can both serve your community and explore your career interests. For example, if you're interested in being a social worker, perhaps you can fulfill your requirement by volunteering at a social service agency and developing a mentor program for refugee students from different countries. Or if you're interested in politics, perhaps you could work with the Registrar of Voters and help set up a program to register students who have just reached voting age.

> In high school, I wish I'd known there were more options beyond doctor, lawyer, or businessperson. I also wish I'd known that you never have to choose what you are going to do forever. You can always change.
>
> —ALICE PRAGER, marketing manager, age 29

Extracurricular Activities

Besides being fun and a great way to make friends, extracurricular activities can also help you explore career possibilities and develop valuable skills. Band, choir, drama, sports, service- or interest-based clubs (for example, language, math, business, teaching), student government, and other activities can provide opportunities to test out your interests and hone your skills. For example, if you think you'd like to teach music, perhaps your band or choir director would let you rehearse a new piece of music with the freshman choir or band. Or if you'd like to be an accountant, taking on the responsibilities of treasurer for a club would allow you to track income and expenditures, create a budget, collect dues, and so on. If you're active in drama, perhaps you could write and direct a one-act play. Serving as an officer of a club, a class, or the student body will help you develop both leadership and people skills.

If you have a particularly supportive and encouraging teacher, club adviser, band or choir director, coach, or other faculty member in an extracurricular activity, talk with that person. Ask what you can do to learn more about jobs related to that activity and how you can develop skills that could be valuable in the work world.

Part-Time or Summer Work

You may get conflicting messages about whether or not you should work while you're in high school. Some people, like economist Steve Hamilton, believe you should put all your energy into your studies and get good grades. According to Dr. Hamilton, "Students get more long-term benefit from improving their grades than they do from a job at Arby's. Employers are looking for signals that a young person is motivated and ambitious. Grades are one signal."

Other people believe that working part-time or in the summer can help you develop important time-management, social, and job skills as well as a sense of responsibility. In some cases, family financial circumstances may require that you work while in high school. If you want or need to work, use your job to develop skills that you can use elsewhere. Even better, find a job in one of the areas you're most interested in, if possible. For example, if you work in a fast-food outlet, develop valuable skills in working with the public. If you have a good supervisor, ask him or her to teach you some basic supervision skills. If you're interested in child development, look for work at a child care center. Instead of taking a part-time job just to earn money, use it to learn skills that will help you find your dream job in the years to come. In addition, save at least a third of your paycheck if you can. Teenagers typically spend 98 percent of what they earn. Spending beyond our means has gotten our country and its citizens into huge financial messes. If you are able to save one or two thousand dollars from your high school jobs, you'll have the money for necessary tools— from funding your college textbooks to taking a trip to check out a potential employer or attend a professional conference.

Savvy Academic Choices

In high school, you have to meet certain academic requirements, but you often have some choice as to how you fulfill those requirements—and you usually have the freedom to choose your electives. Making savvy academic choices can help you land your dream job. If you think that you'll be going to college, check with your college adviser (or a college that interests you) to schedule the high school courses that will be most beneficial to you when you get to college. For example, taking certain AP (advanced placement) or language courses may actually fulfill college requirements and enable you to begin work on your major sooner, and maybe even finish college sooner.

But what if you're not that clear about your future? Here are some ideas that will help you no matter what you decide to do after high school:

- Keep your grades up. Strive to get the best grades you can. When you get your report card, ask yourself, "Did I do the best I could in every class?" If not, up your effort.

- Language skills are very valuable. In addition to English, the languages of choice in the business world are Spanish and Chinese. If you're interested in working in business, seriously consider taking Chinese if your school offers it. Spanish can be useful in many fields—teaching, social service, building and construction, and others. If your school offers Spanish, consider taking it every year.

- If one of your goals in life is to get a well-paying job, take math and science classes. Many challenging careers and high-paying jobs rely heavily on math and science. If your school doesn't have good teachers in these areas, find a tutor or teach yourself using a self-help math book. A librarian or knowledgeable salesperson at a bookstore can give you suggestions about books that are popular and easy to use.

- Broaden your horizons by learning more about your community, your country, and the world. Through your church or a community service organization (like the Lions Club or Rotary), you may be able to find volunteer projects at home and abroad.

- Talk to adults you know and respect. Ask them how they came to do what they're doing. Find out what they like and don't like about their work. Ask if there's anything they wish they had known or done (in high school or later) that would have affected what they're doing today.

Developing Job-Search Skills and Creating a Career Portfolio

By doing the exercises in this book, you've already started developing your job-search skills, a process that will continue throughout your years of work. Particular job-search skills—skills for information and job interviews, expanding your contacts, writing cover letters and thank-you notes—build on the groundwork you laid in the Discovery Exercises in part 1. These concrete skills will help you pursue your career goals and find your dream job. (They may even help you land a good part-time or summer job while you're in high school.) Good job-search skills make the job search easier and more efficient as well as more effective.

If your high school or public library has a career center, check it out—it's a good place to build your job-search skills. Find out what resources the center offers. Does it have classes on resume writing, preparing for job interviews, using social networking, or writing cover letters and thank-you notes? If so, take advantage of them. Talk with the career center staff about your interests and goals. They know a lot about careers and jobs and can point you to helpful resources and opportunities. If you don't have access to a career center, use the Internet and the relevant resources and websites listed in this book.

Here are a few other things you can do to develop your job-search skills and increase your awareness of the world of work:

> Visited an In-and-Out Burger restaurant lately? Every member of the team is fully engaged and treats customers with courtesy. I'm hiring a kid that has those skills. I won't fret too much about their GPA.
>
> —JIM ASCHWANDEN, Rancher and Executive Director, California Agricultural Teachers' Association

- Listen to guest speakers and ask them how they got into the work they're doing.

- Attend career days.

- Continue exploring job possibilities: visit friends or relatives in job settings, develop new contacts and conduct information interviews, or do volunteer work in an area that interests you.

- Attend open houses at community colleges or local universities. Tell college representatives about your interests and ask about possible majors—and prerequisites for those majors—or training programs.

- Go to conferences or meetings of professional organizations that happen near you. Contact the membership officer of professional organizations to find out when the meetings are and if you can come as a guest. As a high school student, you may be able to attend conferences for free.

Job Shadowing

You can learn more about jobs that fit your interests and skills by job shadowing—which means following a person doing a particular job for a day. You might shadow a business executive, a nurse, an architect, a teacher, or an actor. You see everything they see and do: sit in on meetings, phone calls, or contacts with clients or agents; watch them work at the computer or design table; listen to how they teach math to third-graders or prepare their lines for a performance. Job shadowing gives you a real feel for what the day-to-day work is like in a particular profession or job. It also lets you experience the work environment firsthand, which helps you figure out whether you'd like to work in that particular setting all the time.

Job shadowing can be either informal or formal. In the case of informal shadowing, you simply ask a parent, acquaintance, or someone you've done an information interview with if you could shadow them to learn more about their work. Start with a half day—that's much easier on the person you are shadowing. If the work really interests you, ask for additional time on another day that works for them.

Formal job shadowing is usually done through a school, career center, or other organization. The National Job Shadow Coalition, for example, is a joint effort of America's Promise, Junior Achievement, the U.S. Department of Education, and the U.S. Department of Labor. Their yearlong shadowing effort kicks off on Groundhog Day (February 2) each year. Throughout the United States, students shadow workplace mentors to see what different jobs entail and how what they're learning in school relates to the workplace. Past workplace mentors include former president George H. W. Bush, former secretary of state Colin Powell, Monster CEO Jeff Taylor, and *Today Show* anchor Matt Lauer, Al Roker,

PARACHUTE TIP

It's impossible for you to pick a single job for the rest of your life—whether you want to or not. The world of work is changing too much for you to possibly choose a job that will last your entire life. The Occupational Outlook Quarterly reported that you will probably have ten different jobs between the ages of eighteen and thirty-eight. And at age thirty-eight you will likely be in the workforce at least another thirty to thirty-five years. We mention this to reinforce that by doing career planning, you are not picking a job for life. First, you'll want to learn what you want to do to earn a living when you leave school, whenever that is.

and Ann Curry. (For more information on the Job Shadow program and job shadowing in general, see the resources section at the end of this chapter.)

Job shadowing is an excellent way to check out jobs that might match your parachute, particularly your potential dream jobs. You also may find someone who would be willing to be your mentor in a particular field. Mentors are so helpful, you'll probably want more than one. Mentors can help you recognize and develop the skills you have that will be most valuable in a particular field as well as give you guidance on the education or training you'll need, including an appropriate college major. Mentors may also provide valuable contacts for summer employment in the field while you're going to school or contacts for landing a full-time job when you're ready for that. Mentors may give you references when you're job hunting and continue to guide you in your early (and later) days on the job. A good mentor is invaluable; he or she will share a wealth of experience, wisdom, insight, and practical knowledge with you—much of which you're not likely to learn in school. Every time you talk with a mentor, be sure to follow up with a thank-you note.

Internships

Through internships, high school students can gain practical experience in a supervised setting. Generally, an internship runs for several weeks or months so that the intern can learn specific skills or procedures. Internships at the high school level are usually unpaid, although there are some summer programs that do provide salaries. But internships aren't about money. They're about learning valuable skills that will make you more employable or provide you with firsthand information that will help you make sound decisions about your career goals. If you do well, your internship can also gain you business contacts and employment references.

Your high school guidance counselor or career center may know about formal internship programs to which you can apply. Adult members of your school's booster club or local service clubs may also help you find an internship. Check with your local chamber of commerce. They may sponsor internships with local businesses, or they might help you set one up. You may also be able to find internship opportunities through the Internet.

With the help of a parent, teacher, or school adviser, you can set up your own internship. Identify a local business or agency where you'd like to work. Meet with the owner or the manager for the department in which you'd like to work. Ask if they're willing to let you be an intern.

An internship proposal should be in writing. It should list the skills you hope to learn, the duration of the internship, the days and hours you need to be present, and who will supervise you during your internship. Employers think of internships as jobs, and you should too. If you're lucky enough to get one, show up every day on time and willing to learn.

You'll find more about internships after high school in chapter 6.

Creating a Career Portfolio

A career portfolio is a collection of information you've gathered on various jobs and careers as well as information on your interests, skills, and potential dream jobs. It's like your parachute but with more details. Your portfolio can be as simple as a large envelope or a file folder in which you store all the information you've gathered, or you can put your portfolio on your computer. A career portfolio shows what you can do, as well as what you know.

If you go to a high school that offers a career-planning class, you may create a career portfolio as a class assignment. If your high school doesn't have a career class but does have a career center, ask if someone on the staff can help you create a career portfolio. Even if your school doesn't have a career center, you can still put together a career portfolio on your own. Do an Internet search using the phrases "creating a career portfolio" or "creating an eportfolio." (You can also check out *Creating Your Career Portfolio*, by Dr. Anna Williams and Karen Hall, or consult the resources section at the end of this chapter.)

What goes into a career portfolio? Here are a few specific items, but don't hesitate to add anything else you think is important:

- A copy of your filled-in parachute (see My Parachute, page v)

- A list of activities, class assignments, and experiences that show your interest in different jobs

- A copy of the best work that you created for those assignments (if your project is three-dimensional, take a picture of it)

> **THE IMPORTANCE OF OPTIONS**
>
> Less than half of those who start college finish their degree. Given the odds, it's good to have checked out other options for gaining the career preparation necessary for the work you hope to do.

- Information on the education or training you'll need for jobs you're interested in (including recommended college majors)

- Copies of awards, commendations, or certificates from specialized training

- Notes from information interviews

- A list of contacts (for information interviews, job shadowing, and so on)

- Newspaper clippings or magazine articles on people with jobs that you find interesting

This portfolio contains a lot of valuable stuff. If you have an interview for a job or internship, select the parts of your portfolio that best illustrate your skills and experience for the job. And here's a tip: limit yourself to the top three examples of your work. If you take your whole portfolio, you can expect to see your interviewer's eye glaze over.

Keep updating your portfolio throughout high school. You may find that your interests and potential dream jobs change as you do additional research. That's good—that means you're taking your research seriously. But always keep the research you've already done. You never know when a contact you've made or an interview you've conducted in the past may be important. And you may also find new avenues—potential dream jobs—for using your best skills and favorite interests.

Developing a Three-Part Plan

Another helpful thing you can do is to make a three-part plan based on your answers to the following questions. Using your parachute and the section entitled My Favorite Interests (page v), determine your favorite field; that is, the area in which you would most like to find work. Then do additional research (at a career center, library, or online) to answer these questions:

- What entry-level job (a job you can get with a high school diploma) could I get in my favorite field that would help me get experience for better jobs in this field?

- What job could I get in my favorite field with two years (or less) of further training or education?

- What job could I get in my favorite field with a bachelor's degree or advanced training?

You should know the answers to these questions by the middle of your senior year (if not before). To produce some good answers, you may need to return to the people with whom you did information interviews. Remember that each of the questions may have more than one answer—that is, more than one possible job. That's great—it means you have more options. Right now you want as many options as possible, and you want to know what those options are. Having just one choice is very limiting. A one-choice plan is like a one-legged stool—it's almost sure to let you down! When you have the answers to these questions, add them to your career portfolio. The information you gather will help you design a plan for what to do after high school.

Should I Go to College—or Not?

This question sounds quite simple, but given the realities of today's work world, it's more complex than it seems. It used to be that getting a college education generally meant that you would get a better, higher-paying job. That isn't necessarily the case anymore.

To make career plans today, it's important to understand the difference between higher education and training. Higher education is any formal learning you do after graduating from high school, although some people use the phrase "higher education" to mean college or university. If a teacher or career coach suggests higher education, ask them what they mean. Misunderstanding can easily result if you are thinking *technical institute* when you hear the phrase, and they are thinking *state university*.

In general, "education" is a broader type of learning. For example, to get your high school diploma, you have to take certain classes—some interest you, and others don't. To get a college degree, you select a certain major, which should be the subject that most interests you. You're also required to take classes in other subjects to meet graduation requirements. You may or may not find these other classes interesting, though they could provide you with

REALITY CHECK

In our survey of high school and college graduates, 34 percent said that they wish they hadn't waited until they graduated to make career plans and contacts. These former students felt that if they had gotten entry-level jobs, internships, or volunteer experience in fields of their choice while still in school, they would have realized their career goals much faster.

exposure to ideas, issues, and knowledge that may be beneficial personally or professionally.

On the other hand, "training" is more focused or specialized. Training classes teach specific skills, technology, or procedures for use in particular settings and with particular jobs.

The way in which you get your education or training is also rapidly changing. There are many more opportunities today to meet educational or training requirements online or with more flexible learning schedules (for example, weekend or night degree programs).

Whether you choose to prepare for a career or job by going to college, pursuing specialized training, or a combination of the two depends very much on what you want to do. This is where all the research you've been doing on jobs—including the education and training requirements for those jobs—pays off. It can help you make good decisions concerning your further education or training.

Look at your answers to the questions in the previous section, Developing a Three-Part Plan. For each job that interests you and that requires additional education or training, answer these questions:

- What kind of education or training was recommended by the people with whom you did information interviews?

- How long would these studies or training take?

- What will the training for higher-level jobs cost?

- How are you going to pay those costs?

According to the Department of Labor, 75 percent of today's jobs require some amount of education after high school. This is a big change from when your parents graduated from high school and there were more jobs for high school graduates that paid well. But not all good jobs need a university degree. Only 20 percent of today's jobs need a bachelor's degree or higher. Think jobs of the future will need more university graduates? The Monthly Labor Review projects that by 2016, only 22 percent of jobs will require a bachelor's or higher degree. In the four to six years it takes to get a bachelor's degree (only 30 percent of university grads get their degree in four years), a particular technology may have already undergone two or three generations of change. For many employers, the degree process is too slow. They need workers with a technical skill base who can quickly learn more technical skills. Therefore, in some industries, one- or two-year technical degrees are more valued than bachelor's degrees.

Believe it or not, you don't have to go to college to become financially successful. The Census Bureau reports that in the United States, only 30 percent of adults over age twenty-five have a college degree. Many people are financially successful without a college degree. In fact, a passionate interest may be a better indicator of financial success.

The late Srully Blotnick, a PhD in business psychology, decided to find out what happened to people who decided to "go for the money." He studied the career choices and financial success of fifteen hundred people, who were divided into two groups. Group A (83 percent of the people in the study) chose a career because they believed they could earn a lot of money doing it. Group B (17 percent of the study group) chose a career because of their passion and desire for that work. Who do you think made more money?

Twenty years later, 101 of the fifteen hundred had become millionaires. One hundred of them were from group B, those who made choices based on passion. Only one millionaire was from group A, those who chose their career to make money. This means that you are one hundred times more likely to be financially successful if you do work you enjoy. Now, of course, there's nothing that says you can't combine college and your passion. College can be a good place to find and develop your passion and then hone your skills for taking your passion out into the world. College can also be a good place to build a network of friends and acquaintances who can help you pursue your passion professionally.

> If success is defined as getting high-skill/high-wage work—and for most teens this is at least part of the definition—then a prerequisite is gaining an understanding of what they need to compete for good jobs. Is a degree enough? No, it is no longer enough.
>
> —PROFESSOR KENNETH C. GRAY, author of *Getting Real: Helping Teens Find Their Future*

"But I'm not sure what my passion is or what work I want to do," you say. "Should I go to college or not?" Although it is possible to go to college without being certain what you want to do when you get out, it's not advisable, especially if you haven't been academically strong in high school. Even students with A averages have difficulty completing bachelor's degrees. Again, on average, over 50 percent of all teens fail at their first attempt at higher education. About half of that 50 percent drop out between their sophomore and junior year. Why then? Because they don't know what major they want to declare.

If you do make it through and get a degree, if you had no idea what you wanted to do when you started college, odds are you'll graduate the same way.

Is this a bad thing? Usually. The good jobs for college grads have most often been taken by those who had clear career goals. By their sophomore year, students with career focus generally have summer jobs or internships that give them good experience and add to their network of contacts. If you come out of college with over $30,000 in debt and no job prospects, life gets very stressful.

Students tend to think that college will be this wonderful time of exploring their interests and finding job opportunities to match. Community colleges do usually have students take assessments or a career planning course to guide their studies. But, in all higher education, the reality is that you will have to actively seek out these experiences, and the majority of students do not. About one in every three students enter and graduate from their university without having a clue what they are going to do with their education. When questioned, it becomes clear that they did not seek career advice or planning. The "wait and see what I fall into" game has been a great boon for coffee houses seeking baristas. Since only a third of liberal arts graduates (and just half of grads from all majors combined) get jobs that need their education, there are a lot of college grads doing jobs that don't have anything to do with their interests or education. They gripe "I got a degree for this?" Yes. Just imagine what you could be doing if you'd created a good plan for using your education.

> A lot of so-called blue collar trade jobs are now more highly paid than a lot of white collar jobs. So, if we're talking about worthwhile jobs that are interesting, challenging and well paid, then that sort of white collar/blue collar distinction is not a very good indication, any longer, of what goes on in the labor market.
>
> —The Honorable MICHAEL CULLEN, New Zealand Minister of Higher Education and Finance

Most students would be wise to start their higher education at a community college. It can be near where you live now or near the university to which you hope to transfer. In most cases, the first two years are spent meeting general requirements, allowing you to explore many different subjects. Community colleges encourage career exploration. That exploration may help you find fields that fascinate you and identify work that appeals to you. You can then choose a major accordingly. If you do want to go on to get your bachelor's degree, make sure you take classes that will transfer.

You can also take your education in stages. While in high school, see if there are Tech Prep classes you can take. Studies show that students who participate in Tech Prep programs are more likely to graduate from high school, more likely to go on to college, and more likely to get a college degree. Tech Prep and similar career tech programs let you explore an occupation and get skills that will help you support additional studies with jobs that pay well. Since 84 percent of college students work, a job that pays more than minimum wage lets you work less and study more. If your high school doesn't have Tech Prep classes, after you are sixteen you can probably attend community college while still in high school. Or, after you graduate, obtain an associate of arts degree or a certificate that increases what you can earn. Work a while, then go to school for a while. You may have to go through this cycle several times until you achieve your ultimate career goal. This is called an "education ladder." (For a short video on education ladders, visit www.igot2know.com/index .php?videoid=782&partnerid=34.) For generations, this option for achieving educational goals has been chosen by students who are ambitious but do not have a plump pocketbook. For some careers, you must have a bachelor's degree. If that's true for you and you really want to start at a university, be sure to check out scholarships and grants that may enable you to do just that with less borrowed money.

> Where you go after high school, whether you go to college and which college you go to, is much less important than *what* you study.
>
> —RICH FELLER, PhD, author of *Knowledge Nomads and the Nervously Employed*

It's also important to remember that college isn't just studying and going to classes. The social and cultural aspects—making new friends from different parts of the country and the world, attending special events, enjoying the arts—also have an impact on your whole life. Friends you make in college often remain friends—and potential job-search contacts—for life.

As you can see, there are many factors to consider when deciding whether or not to go to college. The answer isn't an easy yes or no. It's important to remember, though, that the choice you make today doesn't prevent you from making another choice later. If you choose to go to work right out of high school, you can still go to college later—although if you have a family of your own that may present a new set of challenges.

Your career goals and work experience—as well as your determination to finish college—can enhance your college experience. If you begin college and find that technical training is more appropriate for the work you want to do, you can switch to a technical program. However, if you've done information interviews, ideally you've learned whether a college degree or training is the best career preparation as well as which particular college degree or type of

For generations, young people moved their socioeconomic status upward through higher education. They pursued degrees that would allow them to enter professions: medicine, criminal justice, education, science, engineering. This may still be a good strategy. The ideal is to have very little debt from earning your first degree. Anyone hoping to go to graduate school must also keep borrowing within manageable limits. Students who have too much debt from earning their undergraduate degree may be denied entrance into graduate programs. For information on college debt, see chapter 6.

training you should pursue. According to Ken Gray's *Getting Real*, one-third of college freshmen drop out within the first three weeks. Few get refunds on tuition or dorm fees, so several thousand dollars can be lost. Information interviews can help you save lots of money and help you make choices you will stick with.

Many people complete college degrees and then return for additional education years later—either to update their knowledge and skills in the field in which they work or to move into another line of work. Occupational skills don't stay current without additional studies or training. To stay highly employable, plan on refreshing or adding to your skills at least every five years. In some fields, you'll need to take additional classes every year.

Another change in the workforce that may affect your career goals is that some technician-level jobs have salaries that exceed professional-level jobs. If you don't mind a year or two of further study after high school but don't like the idea of devoting four to six years, check out technician jobs in fields or industries that interest you.

Remember that you always have options. Even if you later feel you've made a wrong decision, you can choose another direction for your life and work.

Postscript: Life after High School

As we mentioned earlier, in today's work world most well-paying jobs require some amount of additional education or training after high school. You can continue your studies soon after you graduate from high school or wait a couple of years. You may not be ready for college or advanced technical training now, but after a few years of work, you may look forward to going back to school. People who decide to return to school after they've worked for several years often become great students. They have valuable work and life experience, and they've become quite clear on what they want in life—so they go for it!

In choosing what to do after high school, you have many opportunities and possibilities. Here are a few:

- Travel—around the country or around the world.

- Get a part-time or full-time job and continue your education (go to a two-year or four-year school, take online courses, get a technical certificate or license, or learn a skill or trade).

- Get a part-time job and do volunteer work to learn more skills and to make contacts that will help you in your job search.

- Get any job you can to learn more about a particular field or industry.

- Check out a new city or state (or even country!) to live in.

- Begin a government apprenticeship.

- Get a fun job, even if it's not what you want for a career.

- Join the Peace Corps, State Conservation Corps, Job Corps, or Ameri-Corps. Information about these organizations is available at www.bls.gov/opub/ooq/2000/fall/art03.pdf.

- Work or study abroad.

- Join the military.

Does reading this list—or looking at the drawing on the next page—give you more ideas? Add them to the list. What are your top three choices? Whatever you choose to do, do it with your whole heart and live your life to the fullest.

TIRED OF SCHOOL?

After twelve years of classes, no one can blame you if the thought of additional studies doesn't thrill you. However, with unemployment high among young adults (over 25 percent as of this writing), a technical certificate or license, which might take only a few months to finish, can greatly boost your earning potential. If you can't face another day of school, consider a "gap year." You might not want to take a whole year or you might take two. This gap isn't a vacation paid for by your parents; this is a focused time-out. It's time you can work, volunteer, do an internship, or take a few classes so that you learn what you need to know to make better career plans. To learn more, visit www.igot2know.com/index.php?videoid=785&partnerid=34.

Career Portfolios

Social networking sites are gradually becoming capable of serving as electronic portfolios. For example, on LinkedIn you can post slides of your work or presentations. You can also post your work on Google Docs and create a link to your LinkedIn page. Here are some additional resources:

Robins, Mary. *Guide to Portfolios: Creating and Using Portfolios for Academic, Career and Personal Success.* Prentice Hall, 2009.

Here you can try out an eportfolio free for a month (after that, individual accounts are priced based on memory size): **www.eportfolio.org**.

Careers

Crawford, Matthew. *Shop Class as Soul Craft: An Inquiry into the Value of Work.* Penguin, 2009.

Eikleberry, Carol. *The Career Guide for Creative and Unconventional People*, 3rd ed. Ten Speed Press, 2007.

Farr, Michael, LaVerne L. Ludden, and Laurence Shatkin. *300 Best Jobs without a Four-Year Degree*, 3rd ed. JIST Works, 2009.

Gray, Kenneth C. *Getting Real: Helping Teens Find Their Future*, 2nd ed. Corwin Press, 2008.

———, and Edwin L. Herr. *Other Ways to Win: Creating Alternatives for High School Graduates*, 3rd ed. Corwin Press, 2006.

Krumboltz, John D., and Al S. Levin. *Luck Is No Accident: Making the Most of Happenstance in Your Life and Career.* Impact Publishers, 2004.

Nemko, PhD, Marty. *Cool Careers for Dummies,* 3rd ed. For Dummies, 2001.

Phifer, Paul. *Quick Prep Careers: Good Jobs in 1 Year or Less.* Ferguson Publishing, 2002.

Rich, Jason. *202 High Paying Jobs You Can Land without a College Degree.* Entrepreneur Press, 2006.

U.S. Department of Labor. *Young Person's Occupational Outlook Handbook*, 6th ed. JIST Works, 2007.

For information about high-earning jobs that don't require a bachelor's degree, check out this article: **www.bls.gov/opub/ooq/2004/winter/art01.pdf**.

The Internet Public Library's Teen Space offers valuable information on a variety of topics, from lifestyle to money to careers: **www.ipl.org/div/teen/**.

This very popular site includes information on career planning, choosing a college, and job hunting: **www.quintcareers.com/teens.html**.

Project Lead the Way offers classes and projects for middle and high school students interested in exploring engineering and biomedical sciences: **www.pltw.org/index.cfm**.

For interviews with a handful of people who are tops in their field, see this site: **www.streaming futures.com**.

College students have interviewed people about their jobs and how they have or haven't used their college majors. Find out what they learned at this site: **www.roadtripnation.com**.

In short videos, community college students discuss their career decision making and choice of major at: **www.whodouwant2b.com**.

The Bureau of Labor Statistics' Occupational Outlook Handbook site gets you to the latest edition of this always useful resource. The Handbook lists descriptions of thousands of occupations from A to Z. Revised every two years, the handbook describes what workers do on the job. Included are descriptions of working conditions, the training and education needed, earnings, and expected job prospects in a wide range of occupations. **www.bls.gov/oco**

College: Selection and Admission

Asher, Donald. *Cool Colleges for the Hyper-Intelligent, Self-Directed, Late Blooming, and Just Plain Different,* 2nd ed. Ten Speed Press, 2007.

For a book that helps students and their families through the admissions process without killing each other, get a copy of this excellent book: Goodman, Steven, and Andrea Leiman. *College Admissions Together.* Capital Books, 2007.

Nemko, Marty. *The All-in-One College Guide.* Baron's Educational Series, 2004.

North, April. *College Is for Suckers: The First College Guide You Should Read.* iUniverse.com, 2009.

This link will take you to the website of the College Board, the organization that administers the PSAT and SAT tests. It offers advice on getting ready to go to college, financing college, and choosing a college, as well as information on distance learning. **www.collegeboard.com/?student**

In addition to career assessments and information, EUREKA also lists colleges and information about financial aid: **www.eureka.org**.

This site suggests you begin planning for college in the eighth grade (an opinion shared by many): **http://mappingyourfuture.org/MiddleHighSchool**.

This website provides links to all colleges in the United States and its territories: **www.utexas.edu/world/univ/state**.

This website has links to the home pages of all U.S. colleges and universities that grant bachelors or advanced degrees, links to U.S. community colleges and Canadian and other international institutions: **www.clas.ufl.edu/au/**.

For links to home pages of higher education institutions in 194 countries, visit this site: **www.braintrack.com**

If you're interested in distance learning or degrees online, check out this site: **www.online degrees.com**

General Education and Training

Teens with a strong Christian faith may want to check out *Real Life Begins after High School: Facing Your Future without Freaking Out,* by Bruce Bickel and Stan Jantz (Vine Books, 2004).

From 2003 through 2005, the October issue of *Atlantic* magazine contained their annual College Admissions Survey. The articles cover issues important to students who are considering going to college (and to their parents).

This Department of Labor website helps students identify training, educational opportunities, and financial aid. It also tracks occupational and industry trends and provides links with job-search services. **www.careeronestop.org**

Dr. Marty Nemko, a brilliant career strategist and author, offers numerous articles on education and training (including the provocative "College: America's Most Over-Rated Product") on his website: **www.martynemko.com**.

Explore technical careers, check out the skills employers really want, find training, research technical topics, and take a look at the current job market, at the Vocational Information Center site: **www.khake.com**.

Internships

This site provides information on co-op and internship opportunities for high school students: **people.rit.edu/gtfsbi/Symp/highschool.htm**.

This site explains why you should look for an internship in high school: **www.fastweb.com/college-jobs-internships/articles/205-internships-for-high-school-students**.

You can find additional sites dealing with internships by using any search engine. Search on "high school internships" and you'll get pages of options.

Job Opportunities and Information for Teens

Check out this website for jobs and other opportunities for teens: **rileyguide.com/teen.html**.

Teen workers are the most vulnerable to accident and harassment. Provided by the Occupational Safety and Health Administration (OSHA), this is the premier site for teen worker safety and health information. OSHA's mission is to help teen (and adult) workers stay healthy and safe while on the job. **www.osha.gov/SLTC/teenworkers/index.html**

In the United States, restaurants and other eating and drinking establishments employ over three million people under age twenty. Many teens' first work experience is in the restaurant industry. This fun OSHA website helps youths working in the restaurant industry to be safe and healthy on the job: **www.osha.gov/SLTC/youth/restaurant/**.

Job Shadowing

For information on Groundhog Job Shadow Day or the National Job Shadow Coalition, check out this site: **www.jobshadow.org**.

A great article on the whys and how-tos of job shadowing: **www.groovejob.com/resources/sondra-clark-job-shadowing/**.

Again, an Internet search using the phrase "job shadowing for teens" or "job shadowing for college students" will give you pages of links.

National Disability Mentoring Day is usually scheduled every October. Students with disabilities have the opportunity to be matched up with mentors to explore their career interests. To learn more about the program, visit these sites: **www.dol.gov/odep/programs/dmd.htm** and **www.dmd-aapd.org**.

Life Planning and Teen Success

Levine, MD, Mel. *Ready or Not, Here Life Comes*. Simon and Schuster, 2006.

Leslie, Roger. *Success Express for Teens*. Bayou Publishing, 2004.

Benson, Peter. *What Teens Need to Succeed: Practical Ways to Shape Your Own Future*. Free Spirit, 1998.

Mentors

For a site devoted to web-based mentoring for teens, visit **http://netmentors.org**.

This site has general information about mentoring. Enter your zip code to find programs in your area: **www.mentoring.org**.

Articles on subjects ranging from how to select high school classes to Senioritis to balancing school and work can be found at this site: **www.collegeboard.com/student/plan/high-school/index.html**.

Miscellaneous

Education in the United States emphasizes academic intelligence, but there are other kinds of intelligence. One is emotional intelligence—a set of acquired skills and competencies that predict positive outcomes in relationships at home, school, and work. People who possess these skills are healthier, less depressed, and more productive at work, and have better relationships. This site offers a free test that gives a summary of your results and the option to purchase a more detailed report on your EQ: **www.queendom.com/tests/access_page/index.htm?idRegTest=1121**.

For a good summary of Emotional Intelligence, visit **http://en.wikipedia.org/wiki/Emotional_ intelligence**.

For more: Goleman, Daniel. *Emotional Intelligence: Why It Can Matter More than IQ.* Bantam, 1997.

Young people with AD/HD who would like help discovering fulfilling career options and completing the steps mentioned in this book can check out this site: **www.youthleadershipcareers.com**.

This how-to website for teens and twentysomethings is all video; it includes several videos of Carol Christen, coauthor of this book, explaining important career-choice and job-search topics: **www.igot2know.com**.

Volunteering

Becoming a volunteer helps you gain skills while helping others. There are probably dozens of organizations in your hometown that need volunteers. For ideas visit these sites:

www.dosomething.org

www.bygpub.com/books/tg2rw/volunteer.htm

http://life.familyeducation.com/slideshow/volunteer-work/29594.html

Travel is one of the best gifts you can give yourself. Leaving your hometown to volunteer can be sweet—you'll learn more about your country or the world and more about yourself. If you'd like to both volunteer and get out of Dodge, check out these sites:

www.americorps.gov

www.transitionsabroad.com/listings/study/teen/teen_volunteer_organizations.shtml

6

What Do I Do Next?

MAKING THE MOST OF COLLEGE

If you're ready to go to college, that's great! Ideally, you've arrived at this decision through explorations of yourself and your interests, and you've learned that a college degree (from a community college or university) is a prerequisite for your dream jobs. If you've decided that college is for you or is necessary for your target field or job, this chapter will help you get the most out of the experience.

In previous generations, students often went to college to discover what they wanted to do, and they were generally awarded a job after graduation simply because they had a college degree. But you're living in a different world; today a college degree doesn't necessarily guarantee either employment or high pay. Currently, just half of recent grads with bachelor's degrees have found work that requires their level of education. Only a third of liberal arts grads have found jobs that need their education. The graduates of 2009 entered a very rough economy. Barely 20 percent had found full-time work five months after graduation (and three-quarters of those who did find work had done internships while in college), according to the National Association of Colleges and Employers (NACE). This is not intended to discourage you from going to college if you need a bachelor's degree for the work you want to do. We offer this fact to underscore the need to continue paying attention to your career goals and expanding your contacts while you are still in school. Otherwise, you may find that you have treated your college education like a very expensive lottery ticket—you've spent tens of thousands of dollars for the chance at a good job.

By doing the exercises in part 1, you've gained a big advantage over many students beginning college. You know what's important to you and what you need to do—not simply to find a job after graduation but, more important, to find work you love, which for you means getting a college degree. Many students drop out of college because they are not fully committed to completing their education. Career focus will give you that strong commitment.

College can be an exciting and fun time. You meet new people, face academic challenges, and enjoy new social, cultural, and sports activities. Your college friends may remain friends for life. If you remain serious about finding work you'll love after graduation, then while you are in school you'll want to take classes and participate in programs that help you build valuable skills and develop contacts that will enhance your professional career. Your college years

INVESTING IN YOURSELF AND YOUR LIFE

Higher education is a classic investment—time and money spent now to help you get the qualifications you need to do the work you love in the future. Because higher education (both academic and career preparation) can cost so much, financial analysts suggest that the cost of education or training be analyzed just like any other investment.

How do you analyze higher education costs?

- First, be a smart consumer. Talk with people in the field(s) you hope to pursue. Make sure the education or training you're paying for will actually help you get the work you want.

- Second, examine all risks that could threaten your investment. Financial analysts have identified the following five factors as the most common threats to the value of your education or training:

  Debt

  Unfinished schooling

  Low-paying jobs after graduation

  Not using your college degree

  Changing your major

- Third, determine the ROI (return on investment). What will your education or training cost? What is the starting salary for the jobs you want? How long will it take you to pay off your education debts? Will you earn enough to save, start a retirement account, pay down your student loans, and pay other bills?

can be very rich and rewarding in many ways, but they also require a new sense of responsibility—not only for your personal life but also for your financial life. Your college education is an investment in your future.

The Financial Realities of College

It may seem odd to bring up the topic of finances so early in this chapter, but the financial realities of college affect your life not only while you're in college but also—if you borrow money for school expenses or accumulate credit card debt—after college. (And if your parents are paying for part or all of your education, it affects their lives—and possibly their ability to retire—as well.)

You know, of course, that it costs money to go to college. Many people assume that any and all college degrees mean increased earnings when they join the workforce. Some people will even tell you that you must get a college degree, "no matter what it costs." Don't listen. These well-meaning people won't be the ones paying off your student loans. Unless there is no alternative and you need to borrow only a small amount, avoid private student loans. They are not regulated by the government and don't qualify for federal repayment programs. Private loans have no reasonable cap on the interest and fees you can be charged.

There are many websites at which you can learn about student loans. Some are listed at the end of this chapter. One financial reality you need to know is the probable starting salaries for the jobs you want. Your starting salary determines how much you can afford to borrow to finish your degree or training. Once you know the likely starting salaries for jobs that interest you, take that number, divide it by three, and multiply it by two. The resulting number is the total amount you can afford to borrow. (Here's another case for which the research you've done on your preferred career fields and dream jobs is important. Although you may not know exactly what your salary will be, you'll at least have a ballpark figure.)

SOME STARTING SALARIES FOR RECENT COLLEGE GRADUATES*

Chemical engineering: $64,902
Electrical engineering: $60,125
Computer science: $58,837
Accounting: $48,377
Information sciences: $52,089
Finance: $49,940
Marketing: $43,325
History: $37,861
English: $34,704
Psychology: $34,284

*Averages from the National Association of Colleges and Employers, 2009.

Let's say that both you and your college roommate pay the same tuition, $87,500 total. Completing your degrees takes you both five years at a cost of $17,500 per year. You each borrow $23,000 in student loans. Your roommate graduates with a degree in structural engineering. She accepts a job with an annual salary of $50,745. Your degree is in exercise physiology. The best job offer you've gotten so far is for twenty-one hours a week at $12.25 an hour. You hope to pick up another part-time job and cobble together an annual salary of about $26,000 a year. How does your financial situation compare with that of your roommate? If your first job pays half what your roommate earns, your roommate's student loans will be paid off long before yours will. That $23,000 can double in less than ten years through charges for late or missed payments. If you have to pay $350 to $500 a month on your debt, how will that affect where you live, what car you drive, and what you can afford to do in your free time?

College debt is a major issue for college students and their parents. About a third of college graduates leave school not just in debt but in serious financial difficulty. (According to college officials, more students drop out of college due to debt than due to bad grades.) In today's economy, grads who don't take the time to make career contacts and select job targets before graduation are extremely vulnerable. (We'll look at some specific things you can do to make yourself more marketable later in this chapter.)

> ### THE TWO-THIRDS FORMULA
>
> Don't take on too much debt. Most students would be smart to limit their total borrowing to no more than two-thirds of the annual salary they expect to make in their first year after college. If you're at or near that limit and haven't finished your schooling, consider transferring to a cheaper college or taking a year off to work and pay down your loans.
>
> —LIZ PULLIAM WESTON,
> MSN Money Central

So, with the current financial realities of college in mind, how can you make the most out of your college years, particularly in terms of finding work you'll love? As you did in high school, you'll continue to increase your awareness of the work world and hone your job-search skills. The difference is you'll do these things with more depth—and probably more focus too, because you'll be much closer to the day when you'll need to go out and use that work awareness and those job-search skills to land a good job. Now, instead of writing a report on a job you're interested in, you'll research an issue of concern in the field where you hope to find work. Let's say you want to be an infection control nurse. Instead of writing a report on what a nurse does, you'll research new techniques for infection control in hospitals—research that will be valuable when you apply for jobs as an infection control nurse after college. You can use many of your class assignments for career investigation. Your job-search skills may be put to concrete use as you seek a summer job or internship in infection control. When you do information interviews, the information you gather and the contacts you make may lead to a job after graduation.

But what else can you do to make the most of college? Let's look at your college career in terms of what employers look for in new employees. (Actually, *all* high school graduates, whether college-bound or not, should learn these skills, because they're highly valued by employers.)

> Student debt is something that grew very quickly and under the radar. People need to approach college like they approach purchasing a car. Different people can afford different models. Don't be deterred from going to college, but students need to be smart shoppers.
>
> —ANYA KAMENETZ, journalist and author of *Generation Debt*

Cultivating Qualities, Developing Skills

As you select your classes, major, and extracurricular activities, keep in mind what employers look for in employees. In this section, we'll look at the five most desired qualities and skills.

Communication Skills

Excellent verbal and writing skills make it possible for you to communicate well with colleagues, the public, or clients. If you want to improve your writing or speaking, take a speech class (you can always give a speech on the work you want to do) or consider joining a local Toastmasters group. Take a business communications class. If your college has a learning center that offers help with time management, studying, writing, using a computer, and other important skills, take advantage of the resources there, too.

Honesty and Integrity

Employers want employees they can trust, just as clients, customers, or patients want to be able to trust the people to whom they entrust their business, their money, or their health. Integrity demands that you take responsibility for your

---

WHAT ARE EMPLOYERS LOOKING FOR?

Surveys of employers in the United States report that the following are the most important employee skills:

Extremely Important	Very Important	Important
Communication skills (verbal and written)	Strong work ethic	Leadership skills
Honesty/integrity	Motivation/initiative	Self-confidence
Teamwork skills (works well with others)	Flexibility/adaptability	Friendly/outgoing personality
Interpersonal skills (relates well to others)	Analytical skills	Well mannered/polite
	Computer skills	Tactfulness
	Organizational skills	GPA (3.0 or better)*
	Detail oriented	Creativity
		Sense of humor
		Entrepreneurial skills/risk taker

*Employers don't ignore your GPA, but they see it as mainly a measure of your persistence, commitment, and academic aptitude—how well you can jump through academic hoops. (If, however, you plan to go to graduate, law, or medical school, your GPA will be very important.) This doesn't mean you should ignore your GPA and just coast academically, but if you don't have a stellar GPA, you shouldn't worry that it will prevent you from getting a good job. Do your best academically—and also work on cultivating the qualities and developing the skills that employers consider to be the most important.

actions (or inactions), words, and life. Employers want to know whether you are a person who follows through on what you say you will do. Think of examples from your life that show when you have said you will do something and then followed through, even though keeping your word may have been difficult. Have you ever returned a lost item, even if some part of you wanted to keep it? Have you continued working toward a goal, even when it wasn't easy? On your last job, did you work every day and every shift assigned to you?

> The way we have funded higher education in this country has had the unintended consequence of indenturing an entire generation of students who now comprise the "educated poor."
>
> —ROBERT APPLEBAUM, lawyer and founder of ForgiveStudent LoanDebt.com

At one time or another we all fall short of being completely honest or having integrity. If you find that you have particular difficulty being honest or acting with integrity, seek out assistance through your college counseling center, a trusted adult, or a spiritual adviser. For more about integrity, visit: www.eruptingmind.com/examples-importance-personal-integrity.

Teamwork Skills

If you've ever worked on a class project with a team and one person wanted to run the whole show, you know how frustrating it can be. In the workplace, lack of teamwork is not simply frustrating; it's also costly for the employer.

Seek out opportunities to work on a team. You may do this with class projects or in extracurricular activities such as athletics, drama, journalism, or student government. The more you enjoy an activity, the more likely you will be successful at it. You may find team-based extracurricular activities that deal with your interests, such as robotics, student organizations for international relations, or being part of your school's stagehand or media crew. If you have the opportunity to take a class or workshop in conflict resolution, do it.

Interpersonal Skills

Sometimes interpersonal skills are simply called "people skills." These are skills like being able to make conversation with strangers, welcoming people into new settings, resolving conflicts, and listening to the concerns or problems of others. Interpersonal skills come quite naturally to some people and are more of a challenge for others. If they're a challenge for you, watch people to whom these skills come easily. See whether you can adopt some of their ways of relating to people. Check with the career center or the counseling center at your college for resources or resource people who can help you build stronger interpersonal skills. Throughout your college years, take opportunities to develop these skills; for example:

- Be a dorm proctor or adviser.

- Serve in student government, on the dorm council, or as a club officer.

- Give tours of the campus for prospective students.

- Work with children—and their parents—at the college child care center.

Like many other skills, people skills can take practice—and using them can be fun!

Strong Work Ethic

In general, a strong work ethic means that you're willing to work hard; you're dependable, responsible, and punctual; you take seriously the work you do for your employer, and you do that work as well as you possibly can.

As you do your information interviews and job shadowing in college, observe the work ethic in operation at each place of business. Be aware that what's expected at one place of employment may not be expected at another. You need to find a good fit between your own work ethic and that of your employer. (That's why, when you have a job interview, *you* are actually interviewing the *employer* as much as the employer is interviewing you. You want to see whether this is a place where you want to work, just as the employer wants to find out whether you're the person they want and need.)

PARACHUTE TIP

Although being a team builder, good listener, and great communicator will make you a good employee, if you want to be a CEO, different traits are preferred. When it comes to leading successful companies, executive and organizational skills are most important. The traits that lead to corporate success are attention to detail, persistence, efficiency, analytic thoroughness, and the ability to work long hours.

Let's say you want to be a software developer. In your personal work ethic, you're committed to working hard and conscientiously, but you also want time to relax, be with your family and friends, and pursue other interests. You wouldn't fit in well at a company where you're expected to work eighty hours a week, never take a vacation, and spend any free time you might have talking with colleagues about work.

Your commitment to your college education is an indicator of your work ethic. (This is one area where your GPA may reveal qualities an employer considers valuable.) In general, if you're serious about getting as good an education as possible, you'll study hard and be dependable, responsible, and punctual (that is, you'll meet course requirements and won't cut classes or show up late). You'll take your academic work seriously and do your work as well as you possibly can.

If you need help with study skills, see if your college has a learning resource center. Utilize department assistants or tutors if you need them. If you're having difficulty with a particular class, talk with the professor or teaching assistant to see if you can get some additional help. Your initiative in getting help indicates a strong work ethic.

Contacts

In addition to developing the qualities and skills that employers want most, it's important to use your college years to gain work experience and develop contacts that will be useful to you when you interview for jobs. Information interviews, job shadowing, and internships (sound familiar?) are good ways to gain experience and develop contacts.

Information Interviews and Job Shadowing

Continue doing information interviews as you did in high school, but now do them in more depth. (To review information interviewing and job-shadowing techniques, see chapters 4, 5, and 8.) Ask to meet with people for thirty minutes and ask for more detail about the day-to-day realities of their jobs and the direction they see their career field taking, including what opportunities or obstacles that might present for you.

Chapter 5 offered some basic information about job shadowing. You can use the same technique in college to learn more about particular jobs. With additional life, academic, and possibly work experience, you'll be better able to use the experience to assess whether a particular job is suitable for you.

Ask the staff at your college career center for help in finding people (perhaps alumni) for you to job-shadow or interview. Faculty members in the area of your major, as well as your college roommates and friends (and their parents), may also provide important contacts. Get in touch with your college's office of alumni relations. Most schools have databases about their grads that include employment information. And don't forget those people you job-shadowed or did information interviews with when you were in high school. If your interests still lie in the same area, contact them again to see whether they might be willing to be shadowed or interviewed again—this time in more depth.

Internships

Employers prefer to hire college students who have done multiple internships. They weigh internship experience higher than grades, the college you attended, and even your professional recommendations. Many companies and businesses offer internships to college students. Some are paid and some are not; some take place during the summer, others during the school year. Internships are designed to introduce you to working in a particular field or job and to give you practical work experience. For example, let's say you want to be a magazine staff writer. A magazine may offer a summer internship program that introduces you to the publishing world, allows you to work with a staff writer, and gives you a writing assignment to complete before the end of your internship.

Internships are a great way to check out a job or field that you're very interested in, and they look good on your resume. The quality of internships varies wildly. Some students report being active members of a team; others say that

GET IT IN WRITING

When you finish an internship, volunteer project, or job in which you have done well, ask for a letter of recommendation before you leave. Even if your supervisor or professor likes and remembers you, he or she may have trouble remembering the details of your work after even six months. These letters can be important as recommendations for both jobs and graduate school.

they just warmed a chair. Find students who have already done the internships that interest you. Avoid internships that are a waste of time. Make sure you do your part; show up on time, professionally dressed and open to new assignments. If your experience is a good one, after you graduate you may be offered a full-time position at the business where you interned, or people you worked with may offer to write professional references for you or provide contacts with potential employers.

Check with the career center at your college for information on internships. (Also see the resources section at the end of this chapter.) If you're unable to find an internship that fits your particular needs, try contacting a company that you're interested in working for to see whether you can set up an internship.

You As a Business

Young adults are sometimes referred to as "start-up adults." It's an interesting metaphor, as it alludes to a person in the first phase of business, just starting up. It's also a helpful metaphor. No business would spend $80,000 to $120,000 (what getting a bachelor's degree may cost you) on a new piece of equipment or a service without knowing what it would do for them. Smart college-goers won't either. The goal of your business plan is to leave college with a job you'll like and one that needs your college education. From recent studies, here's what those who achieve this goal do during college:

Summer of freshman year (or earlier): Complete your parachute and do enough information interviews to learn about three fields or industries that interest you. Find out what internships are available through your university. Keep a list of names and contact information of all the people you meet who work in the field you also want to work in.

Sophomore year: Use breaks to investigate those careers further. You want to know which field or industry appeals to you most so that you can

---

ARE YOU BACKABLE?

Venture capitalists look for new businesses (called start-ups) that are likely to succeed. Explore and increase your backability with these two books:

- *Backing U: A Business-Oriented Guide to Backing Your Passion and Achieving Career Success* by Vaughn Evans (Business and Careers Press, 2009)
- *Me 2.0: Build a Powerful Brand to Achieve Career Success* by Dan Schawbel (Kaplan, 2009)

declare a major by the start of your junior year. Students who don't have a clue what they want to do with their major, or who change majors more than once, are more likely to get jobs that don't use their college degree. Apply for summer internships.

Summer of sophomore year: Get an entry-level job or internship in the industry that interests you most or set up a series of volunteer internships in several fields so you can check them out. Update your contact list and your plan for success.

Junior year: Apply for summer internships. Look for professional conferences or local professional association meetings to attend.

Summer of junior year: Secure an internship or job in the field. Update your contact list and your plan for success.

Senior year: Organize your classes so that you can do another internship before you graduate. Get in touch with all your contacts to let them know you are actively looking for work and what you want. Ask them to let you know if they hear of openings. (Seniors who graduate with a job lined up report that it took six to nine months of active job search to secure it.)

The College Experience

Though our focus in this book is on helping you find work you'll love, life is more than just work. The college experience, in addition to providing you with academic grounding for your life's work, also challenges you to discover what you truly value and to find a way to balance the many different aspects of your life. If taken seriously, the challenges and responsibilities that you didn't have to worry about very much while you were living at home will help you grow and mature. These include learning to work out differences with roommates, facing new financial realities (such as using credit and student loans wisely), balancing study time with social time and perhaps work obligations, and maybe maintaining an apartment (cleaning, grocery shopping, and cooking). If you ignore the challenges of college life and just party, you'll waste not only a lot of money but also your opportunity to be better prepared for finding good and satisfying work after college. The new life experiences of college can develop important skills that will help you when you join the work world.

But most of all, enjoy yourself! No time in life is quite like your college years. Have fun, learn as much as you can, and continue building a strong foundation of skills to help you find work you'll love.

Careers

Coplin, Bill. *10 Things Employers Want You to Learn in College: The Know-How You Need to Succeed*. Ten Speed Press, 2004.

Levit, Alexandra. *They Don't Teach Corporate in College*, rev. ed. Career Press, 2009.

Pilate, Victoria. *Dorm Rooms to Boardrooms*. Signature Books, 2004.

This website has great music and stories about people's journies to find their work niche after college: **www.roadtripnation.com**.

This website has job-search tips for college students: **http://jobsearch.about.com/od/ teenstudentgrad/a/collegejob.htm**.

This site offers a variety of career information, including a link to a career quiz: **www.princeton review.com/cte/**.

Geared to college students and recent grads, this site lists both jobs and internship opportunities: **www.monstertrak.com**.

Designed for the University of Waterloo (Canada), this site's comprehensive six-step Career Development eManual includes downloadable worksheets: **www.cdm.uwaterloo.ca**.

College: Selecting Majors or Transferring to Another School

Freedman, Eric. *How to Transfer to the College of Your Choice*. Ten Speed Press, 2004.

At this site you can download a PDF booklet or work online with a humorous video to select a major: **http://missingmajor.com**.

You can purchase an interactive DVD to help you select your college major at **www.careeroptions 4me.com/products.htm**.

This site lists nearly forty majors and some associated careers: **www.collegeboard.com/csearch/ majors_careers/profiles/index.html**.

College: Surviving and Thriving

Carter, Carol. *Majoring in the Rest of Your Life: Career Secrets for College Students*, 4th ed. LifeBound, 2004.

Combs, Patrick. *Major in Success: Make College Easier, Fire Up Your Dreams, and Get a Great Job*. Ten Speed Press, 2007.

Kamenetz, Anya. *DIY U: Edupunks, Edupreneurs, and the Transformation of Higher Education*. Chelsea Green, Spring 2010.

Stafford, Susan. *Community College: Is It Right for You?* Cliff Notes, 2006.

Tyler, Suzette. *Been There, Should've Done That: 995 Tips for Making the Most of College*, 3rd ed. Front Porch Press, 2008.

A highly recommended book for teens and parents from Great Britain, *If I'd Only Known: Making the Most of Higher Education,* is no longer in print. But you can download it in PDF form at the following website (scroll down to near the bottom of the page): **http://www.agr.org.uk/Content/ If-Only-I-had-Known**.

These two articles, written during the last economic downturn, explain the decline in jobs for university grads and the limits of higher education:

http://www.bearcave.com/misl/misl_other/college_grad_unemployment.html

www.epi.org/publications/entry/webfeatures_viewpoints_education_limits/

This site links you to blogs of recent grads going through the frustrations of finding a job: **www.onlinecolleges.net/2009/07/15/100-motivational-blog-posts-for-disgruntled-grads/**.

Financial Realities and Avoiding Debt

Kamenetz, Anya. *Generation Debt: How Our Future Was Sold Out for Student Loans, Bad Jobs, No Benefits, and Tax Cuts for Rich Geezers—and How to Fight Back.* Riverhead Trade, 2006.

Sheer, Marc. *No Sucker Left Behind: Avoiding the Great College Rip-off.* Common Courage Press, 2008.

On the Internet, you'll find dozens of articles about the cost of college, student loans, and credit card debt. Read several so you know what's happening and how to avoid mistakes other students have made.

This website has college finance and credit card calculators so that you can see what your real costs are: **www.bankrate.com**.

Financial Literacy

Duguay, Dara. *Please Send Money: A Financial Survival Guide for Young Adults on Their Own,* 2nd ed. Sourcebooks, 2008.

Feeley, Craig and Lisa. *Spendright: The Smart Start for Students.* CMK Publishing, 2005.

Amanda van der Gulik writes and blogs about teaching children how to make, manage, and save money. You can follow her on Twitter: @AmandavdGulik. Her website is **www.teachingchildrenabout money.com**.

A job finances your life. Here are two websites that show what the lifestyle you want will cost and suggest jobs that earn enough to finance that lifestyle:

www.californiarealitycheck.com

www.jumpstart.org/realitycheck

Internships

For listings of internships, apprenticeships, and volunteer and study-abroad opportunities, check out these sites:

http://rileyguide.com/intern.html

www.aftercollege.com/job-channel/internships

www.quintcareers.com/grad_internships.html

www.campusinternships.com

For more information on internships, do an Internet search using the phrase "college internships."

7

Goal Setting

A TOOL TO SHAPE YOUR FUTURE

As you've been reading through the previous chapters, completing the exercises, and answering questions, you've been gathering information on your interests, skills, and potential dream jobs. This research on yourself has helped you discover more about your likes and dislikes. You've seen how you can use your high school and college experiences to enhance your job readiness and awareness of the work world. This exploration should have given you some ideas about how your interests give shape to your work and your future. Now we'd like to introduce you to a tool that will help you do both. Goal setting helps you discover a bit more about what you want out of life and define how you'd like to spend your time in the future.

A goal is something you want to achieve or accomplish: learning to drive a car, getting a high school or college diploma, or being elected student body treasurer. A goal can also be to experience something you dream of: traveling to India, going white-water rafting, or meeting a relative you've never met. Some of your goals may be personal, such as getting to know someone better, reading a particular book, or learning to get along with your little sister better; others may be academic, like getting into a particular college, earning a 3.0 GPA, or surviving chemistry. Still others, like finding your dream job or getting into a work-training program, may be work-related. Because life is about more than just school or work, your goals can relate to anything—relationships, learning experiences, or just simply having fun.

Goals help us in many ways. Have you ever set a goal and achieved it? What did you learn about achieving a goal through this experience? If you have set a goal, but didn't achieve it, run over the experience in your mind and identify what got in your way that's in your power to change. Failure, well studied, is a great teacher.

Goals help articulate (that is, they help us name and talk about) what we really want to do. They help us define what's most important to do with our time, and how we are going to change how we spend our time to achieve a stated goal. Goals also help motivate us to do what we say we want to do! Just writing goals down makes them more concrete. When we say we want to do something some-day, that "something" and "someday" remain very vague, and more often than not we never get around to doing it. Rather than just talking about something you want to do, knowing your goals and working toward them means you are likely to achieve them. A goal on a list is just an idea unless you put in the effort to achieve it. When you achieve your goals, you feel better about yourself. Life becomes more interesting and you'll feel more in control of your own destiny.

Choosing Goals

Goals have different timelines. For example, you may find it helpful to set three-month or six-month goals—or goals for your academic term. You may have papers to write or projects due during this time. For any given goal, if you make a list of what you need to do month by month or week by week, you can achieve your goal without cramming in all the work at the last minute.

You'll probably want to take more time to think about longer-term goals, such as lifetime goals. It's important to remember that your goals reflect your values. When you think about your goals, ask yourself:

- What is important to me?

- What do I most want to do with my time on earth?

These are not easy questions to answer, but they're important to think about. Some of your goals may change over time while others become clearer. Whenever you accomplish a goal, find another one to take its place.

GOAL SETTING

Take a sheet of paper. Turn it so that the long edge is horizontal and fold it into four equal vertical columns. Draw a line near the top to create one row for column headings. Title the first column "What I hope to do in my life"; the next column, "Things I hope to do in the next one to three years"; and the last column, "If I were to die in six months, how would I want to spend my time?"

Set a timer for two minutes (or have a friend time you). Start with any column. Write down anything that comes into your head during those two minutes. After two minutes are up, set the timer for another two minutes and turn to one of the other columns. It makes no difference which one you do next. Complete all four columns. This whole exercise will take you just eight minutes.

Read over each column. What do you think about the things you've written? Are there any surprises? Were any sections more difficult to complete than others?

Take a look at that last column, "If I were to die in six months, how would I want to spend my time?" What activities did you list? The activities you'd choose if you had little time to live would be those things you value most. Look at your list in that column. Does it reflect what is most important to you?

You probably have things you have to get done in six months or there will be serious consequences (term papers and finals, for instance). But life needs some fun, too. What are some personal goals you'd like to accomplish or get started on in the next six months? Now that you've gained a new perspective on your six-month goals, revise the list to reflect your actual goals for the next six months, both personal and those related to school or career-planning.

It may be a few days before you want to prioritize your goals. Just thinking about things you want to do and experience in your lifetime may stimulate other ideas over the next few days. Add these ideas to the appropriate column, depending on the time frame of the goal. When your list feels complete, prioritize the list so that the items first on your list are the most important to you. Write your two or three favorite goals from each list at the center of your Parachute diagram (page v).

Accomplishing Your Goals: To-Do Lists

A goal without a plan is just an idea. Once you begin to articulate your goals, it's important to plan how you're going to accomplish them. A good way to do this is the simple to-do list. You can also put your goals on a calendar on the dates by which you want them finished.

Let's say that one of your goals is to attend a particular college or art or technical school. Here's what your to-do list might look like:

1. Check out the school's website for admissions and application information.

2. Register to take the SAT (or other admissions tests).

3. Talk to a college admissions counselor about high school courses I should take.

4. Register for those courses.

5. Take the SAT.

Perhaps, as you're working your way through your to-do list, you learn that, because you're going to an art or technical school, you don't have to take the SAT, but you do have to prepare a portfolio for the admissions process. In that case, you'll revise your to-do list to look something like this:

1. Find out the explicit requirements for the portfolio.

2. Talk to the admissions counselor about portfolio requirements and high school courses I should take.

3. Begin assembling my portfolio.

4. Complete my portfolio by the application deadline.

When preparing your to-do list, think of it as breaking down your goal into very manageable steps. If you make the steps too big, you may get discouraged. If the steps are just the right size, you'll keep moving toward your goal. If you find that you keep avoiding your to-do list, maybe you don't really want to achieve this goal—or maybe the steps are too big. Take one step and break it down into two or three smaller steps. Each time you complete a step, check it off. Completing a step is an accomplishment in itself. Each step you complete moves you closer to your goal.

PARACHUTE TIP

If you'd like to see how setting goals for yourself can help you bring about future success, but are unsure how to make it happen, enlist the help of an adult—someone you trust who has achieved a lot of the same goals you have. Together with your goal coach, brainstorm ideas for a very short-term goal—say, a thirty-day goal. Then brainstorm what you need to do every day to achieve your goal. Put those steps on a calendar (one you can't miss, that's either in your face or on your iPhone).

Reevaluating Goals

As you move toward your goal—particularly your long-term goals—you'll have new experiences and gather new information, both about yourself and about your goal. New experiences and information will help you evaluate that goal. Sometimes the experiences you have moving toward a goal are more valuable than achieving that goal. What you learn may confirm that a particular goal is the right one for you, or your experiences may lead you to revise your goal to include new ideas or new life directions. It's okay to let go of a goal when it no longer has meaning for you. Replace it with a new goal that is more important to you.

A Tool for Life

Goal setting isn't something you do just once. You'll find that the types of goals that interest you change over time. You'll continue to set goals (and develop to-do lists to accomplish those goals) all your life. Knowing how to set and achieve goals is a very important life tool. By the goals you set and work toward, you shape your life.

IF YOU WANT TO EXPLORE FURTHER . . .

Bachel, Beverly K. *What Do You Really Want? How to Set a Goal and Go for It! A Guide for Teens.* Free Spirit Publishing, 2001.

Bishop, John. *Goal Setting for Students.* Accent on Success, 2009.

Videos

How to set goals (great information and music beat): **www.youtube.com/watch?v=D7j1ng7C8HI& feature=fvw**.

School program in goal setting: **www.schooltube.com/video/22535/SubDivide-Goal-Programs-for-Students**.

8

Social Networking

USING SOCIAL MEDIA TO BOOST YOUR CAREER

Social media is all about connection, communication, and conversation. Social media sites encourage community building and discussions. Social media differs from commercial media in that content isn't just delivered to passive viewers. Most social media sites ask members to vote, comment, and share information. Site members respond to posts and create content. They can upload comments through software that allows anyone without programming skills to post or form communities around mutual interests.

There are all kinds of social media sites, from news to sharing videos, pictures, bookmarking, and social networking. Social networking expands the number of one's social contacts by making connections through existing friends. Social networking has gone on for millennia, as long as humans have lived in groups larger than extended families.

The Internet has unlimited potential for multiplying connections through web-based groups like Facebook. With the Web, you can bridge the six degrees of separation very quickly. Perhaps you already belong to AvatarsUnited, Goodreads, Quarterlife, or MySpace. If you've used your site to meet people, check in with friends, or find things out, you already know how it feels to have a network. That's a good start. But did you know that you can use social networking sites to explore careers, meet people who do the work that interests you, and uncover internships and even job openings?

Recently, using both traditional social networking sites and sites specifically developed for expanding one's business contacts has become the hot way to recruit new employees and find out about jobs. So here's some basic information about safely using your current social networking site to expand your career awareness, find jobs and information about jobs, and make new contacts for the employment side of your life.

How to Stay Safe Using Social Networking

The point of using a site you belong to now to explore careers is that you are connected to people you trust. Through your site friends it's likely that you'll be able to find out even more information about a field, job, or other career aspect that fascinates you than you'd be to uncover on your own. But before you dash off a post asking about circus jobs, you need to carefully plan how to minimize any risk to yourself. You need to plan how to manage, for your safety, how much access you allow new contacts. What image of you will they see when they contact you? Make a list of your ideas about how you want to look, and what you want to write about yourself and your career search. Which privacy settings will you use on your site?

PARACHUTE TIP

"Social networking" is a technical term for online sites. Online social networking has nothing to do with being social in everyday terms.

To expand your list about how to keep safe and create your online image, talk to friends or ask a teacher whether time can be scheduled for a class discussion. Or get an adult with Internet and social media smarts to read over your list and add suggestions for how you keep yourself safe while exploring this whole new world of information. If, despite your best efforts, someone creeps you out, cease all contact and send all correspondence to one of your parents or an adult you trust. The world is full of wonderful and terrible people. (May you meet far more of the first kind.) You need a plan for online socializing that minimizes the chance of your meeting the second kind.

How to Use Social Networking for Career Exploration

With new applications and features, social networking sites have morphed into sites for job searching and creating a go-to network for career information. To get the most out of them, you'll need to get savvy.

The protocols and applications for using networking sites change so fast that whatever we describe will be obsolete by the time we finish typing this sentence. Well, maybe not that fast, but nearly. New sites and applications for them come out every month. If we walked you through the steps of setting up an account, by the time you read our descriptions the screens wouldn't be the same. The Internet can help you learn more about how to use networking sites for career exploration and job search. Be sure to create an email address appropriate for the business world. Your first and last name run together, first initial and last name run together, or the name of your company if you've started a business are all acceptable. This is not the place to use a silly or risqué nickname.

Here are some helpful phrases for searching the Internet or Wikipedia:

- Using social networking to find a job

- Using social networking to find internships

- Setting up a social network site for job hunting

- Using (put name of specific social network here) for career information or job search

- Job finding online

Pages of links will come up. Look at the publishing dates and read several of the most recent. By using the same networking protocol as you would for an internship or job, you can also find job-shadowing opportunities and people to talk with about their work.

Creating a Solid Web Presence

Here are some tips to get you started.

1. Understand that the Internet is forever. Some people have posted images of themselves on the Web that their grandchildren will see someday. Has that thought ever crossed their minds, or do they really not care? Most adults have had a scrape in their youth that they'd not like to have revealed, much less have it circling the globe into infinity. With the Web, images sent out innocently can come back to hurt.

2. Do a search of your name. See what recruiters or human resource personnel will find if they do the same. About 77 percent of recruiters do web searches of potential applicants. Half of them have used information they've uncovered to eliminate candidates. Recruiters often, but not always, work for large businesses. Assume that small business owners, managers at nonprofit agencies, or workers at education institutions will search for you on the Web too.

3. If possible, set your profile privacy settings so only those you have approved have access to it. Because you can't control what your friends might post, choose to block comments if such a setting is offered. Even if it was a friend—not you—who made an offensive post, it will be seen as a reflection on your character.

4. Ask friends, older siblings, coworkers, parents, and friends' parents whether they have used social or business networking sites for career exploration or job hunting. If they have, you might want to ask for their help setting up your profile or ask to see their profiles as models.

5. When you contact people for career-related reasons (on the Internet or in real time), maintain professional manners at all times. (If you don't know what professional manners are, you need to learn what they are and how to use them. Type the phrase "professional manners" into a search engine and learn from the articles that result.) There's a line between taking initiative and stalking. Make sure you don't cross it, and don't let anyone stalk you. If you've sent a note and not gotten a response, it's all right to send two more notes, each a week apart. After that, you may need a mutual friend to intercede on your behalf or accept that this person is not

going to respond. If someone is sending you multiple messages in a day, and they aren't career related, block their access to you.

As to the image you project to the world, make it appropriate, both for your age and for public viewing. There are dozens of blogs, tweets, and Internet marketing impresarios that can give you ideas about how to craft your brand (that's *you*, by the way). The old rule about having just one chance to make a good first impression takes on a new meaning with social networking. Social networking also lets you feel how small the world has gotten. Join any site and you may be contacted by people from around the world whose interests you share.

Twitter

As if social networking didn't bring enough excitement to the Internet, some bright spark (Jack Dorsey) thought the added challenge of making posts in no more than 140 characters would make blogging even more fun. This micro-blogging began as a way to stay in touch, using posts called tweets to answer the question, "What's happening?" and ended up creating a whole new subset of social media.

Twitter has become the current rage for businesses seeking new ways to advertise. As the popularity of social media grows, traditional advertising on commercial media has become less effective in driving customers to buy

PARACHUTE TIP

On his website, adriandayton.com, lawyer and Twitter guru Adrian Layton has a series of one-minute videos showing how to set up and manage a Twitter account.

products. Twitter has also become very popular as a site through which one can expand career contacts and clients, job-search, and check on current and potential employees.

If you want to try out Twitter, create two accounts. With friends, you can use a playful screen name or avatar. For career exploration or job search, use your real name and a headshot of yourself in a smart blouse, shirt and tie, or jacket. Tie your career Twitter account to an equally professional email address. First initial and last name, both first and last name, your business name, or your interest sector are all commonly used screen names. Your Twitter account for friends can be tied to a different email address.

Sites with a Business Focus

The job hunt is still very much a people-to-people effort. That's one reason job boards like Monster, Yahoo's HotJobs, and CareerBuilder are losing business and being replaced by social networking sites. Social networking relies on people-to-people contacts.

There are a growing number of social networking sites specifically set up to help people achieve their career and professional goals. LinkedIn, Jigsaw, and E.Factor are just a few of the most popular sites. There are plenty more, and new ones appear online all the time.

What's the Difference?

Business sites call themselves social networking sites, but they are much more formal. LinkedIn, Ryze, and Koda are examples of sites that were created for business networking. Their focus is to help members expand their professional contacts and find potential employers (and employees). Using them can give you a professional presence on the Web.

These "professional" sites aren't limited to college grads, and they can help you make some connections for your own future. You will want to learn about them as your career interest builds. Always ask friends, people you work with, and your career mentors about new sites for your field or interests.

Online Resumes and Supporting Documents

Create a great online resume. Take a look at examples of different online resume forms and models. What will work best to show off your abilities? Get help from experienced people you trust. Post recommendations from teachers,

LOOK UP INTERESTING PEOPLE

Select the top five companies you want to work for or want to know more about and search for people working there through LinkedIn and Technorati blogs. There are also people-search engines such Pipl, PeekYou, and Wink. Every time you hear about a company that interests you, a young entrepreneur, or a new process or procedure that someone has invented, look them up and see what you can find out that may help you make career decisions.

a favorite camp counselor, your youth minister or other leader of your spiritual community, and former employers or supervisors from volunteer work or internships.

LinkedIn is currently the most popular site for posting about your career. Here are some of the things you can accomplish on LinkedIn:

Use Google Docs to post term papers, science fair projects, thesis papers, Eagle or other scouting projects, articles, senior projects, or other examples of your outstanding work—anything that relates to your career goals. Then link the Google Docs to your LinkedIn profile. If you have made things, created pictures, or written short stories or poetry, post pictures or documents of these as well.

Make a link from VisualCA.com to your LinkedIn profile. VisualCA.com lets you create and post a resume for free.

Do searches of People, Companies, and Groups. Be sure to join groups that relate to your career interests.

Always Respond!

If you send out a request on LinkedIn or other social networking sites, reply to every single response you get, even if you aren't interested. Blowing people off is a sure way to get blown off in the future. Those who give you the name of someone to contact are risking their reputation with that person. Regardless of your interest, send at least a brief, polite follow-up message to every name you are given. You just never know when an opportunity will appear.

PARACHUTE TIP

Don't ask a new contact for a job. Executives and hiring managers at high-profile (and not-so-high-profile) companies are hit up for jobs all the time. Use your messages to learn about a company or what's happening in a particular field or industry. Introduce yourself and ask questions that will lead to a positive interchange. Once you have a good relationship with your contacts, you can ask more directly about job opportunities—or better yet, they may bring up job opportunities and contacts on their own.

A World of Possibility

The ability to gain career information expanded geometrically with the Internet and expanded many times more with social media. You can use social networking sites to create an online job-search support group, tweet your career action plans to friends, create blogs about your interests, or share your job-search frustrations. To get the most out of using social media sites that are new to you, you will want to go slowly, getting familiar with the sites available. At first, join just one. As you learn more about what you want to find out or accomplish through social networking, you can be more discriminating in the sites you join and spend time on.

Social networking may be the best job-search strategy of the twenty-first century, but the sites you choose and how you use them will determine whether they become an effective career exploration and job-search tool for you. Networking through social media sites is the latest career exploration technique, but something else will replace it eventually. Stay alert for that something else and learn how to use it to boost your career.

IF YOU WANT TO EXPLORE FURTHER...

The brilliant social media diva Patti Wilson gives online classes on how to use social networking sites in your job search: **www.pattiwilson.com/consulting/social-networking/**.

Follow twentysomething personal branding and social networking expert Dan Schawbel on Twitter: @danschawbel.

Penelope Trunk has created both a blog about career and life issues and a social network to help young people manage their careers. You can find both at **http://blog.penelopetrunk.com**.

For a delightfully irreverent take on our dependence on technology see **www.youtube.com/watch?v=I6IQ_FOCE6I**.

Here's a Harvard Business piece, "How Twitter and Crowdsourcing Are Reshaping Recruiting": **http://blogs.harvardbusiness.org/cs/2009/09/how_twitter_and_crowdsourcing.html**.

Try this list of popular social networking sites: **http://en.wikipedia.org/wiki/List_of_social_networking_websites**.

Follow a hundred career blogs (you'll never lack for advice): **www.careerrocketeer.com/2009/07/100-career-blogs-all-professionals-must.html**.

This article gives an overview to the use of social networking sites for job search and offers an example of one man's success: **www.time.com/time/business/article/0,8599,1903083,00.html**.

7 Secrets to Getting Your Next Job Using Social Media: **http://mashable.com/2009/01/05/job-search-secrets/**.

This article gives some guidance on how to use LinkedIn to research companies (the site has a similar article on using Twitter): **www.cio.com/article/480610/How_to_Use_LinkedIn_Company_Profiles_For_Job_Hunt_Networking_**.

Here are twenty social networking sites for business professionals: **www.sitepoint.com/blogs/ 2009/07/28/social-networking-sites-for-business/**.

Find lists of companies that can help people get jobs through Twitter:

http://TweetMyJobs.com

www.TwitJobSearch.com

Learn Twitter lingo: **http://twitterwatchdog.com/2009/10/10/learn-the-twitter-lingo/**.

From marketing genius Guy Kawasaki, a different take on using social networking: **www.openforum .com/idea-hub/topics/the-world/article/how-to-go-on-the-offensive-with-facebook-guy-kawasaki**.

PART THREE

LANDING YOUR DREAM JOB . . . AND MORE

> I wish that someone would
> have told me that success comes
> more easily if you are doing a job that
> you truly enjoy and not to pursue a career
> that seems "safe" if it is going to make you
> miserable. People have said that forever.
> Apparently this needed to be pounded
> into my head.
>
> —JULIE PORTEOUS LEACH,
> auditor, age 29

ARE you ready to learn how to land your dream job? A job that will help you get the experience you need to go after your dream job? Or work that will bring you great satisfaction and help you afford the life you want? Great! All the work you've done in the earlier chapters of this book provides a foundation for this next important step. In part 1, you became a detective in your own life, finding clues that revealed your dream job (or field) by identifying your interests, best skills, favorite types of people, and ideal work environment. In part 2, you explored ways to continue the journey toward your dream job by making the most of high school and higher education, and using tools like goal setting and social networking.

Now we'll dive into the depths of job hunting. First, we explore concrete ways to make your job hunt more efficient, effective, and successful (chapter 9). Then we look at the top ten mistakes job hunters make—and how you can avoid them (chapter 10). Since many of you will find success in careers not yet imagined, next we use green careers to show you the importance of tracking career trends (chapter 11). Finally, we put the search for your dream job in the larger context of your whole life (chapter 12). We invite you to consider who you want to be, what you most want to do in life, and how you can use your talents to make the world a better place to live.

9

How to Search For—and Find—Your Dream Job

Job hunting is both exciting and scary, and probably a few other things as well! But if you've carefully prepared your parachute—named your interests, skills, preferred people and work environments, and ideal salary—you'll be far ahead of most people beginning the job search. Because you've started cultivating your awareness of the work world and developing job-search skills (such as information interviews) in high school, you have a good springboard for diving into the actual job hunt—and finding your dream job.

Good Job versus Dream Job

Let's consider, just for a moment, the difference between a "good job" and a "dream job." A good job is a job that you enjoy most days, that pays well (given your level of skill and the going rate in the marketplace), and that uses many of your best skills. A dream job, on the other hand, is one that you love. It feels like learning, work, and play all rolled into one. You'd do it even if they didn't pay you well. But in a dream job, the pay is good (again, considering both your skills and the marketplace). The job uses at least 75 percent of your best skills, incorporates your interests, and expresses your values. (The identification of these factors as vital to career satisfaction comes from longtime Parachute practitioner Deeta Lonergan.) At various times in your life, you'll need to take a good job. It's as hard to find a bad job (one that's bad for you) as a good one. Go for a good one. You won't work hard at a job you don't like, and it's those who do the equivalent of A- or B-level work who get promoted.

We are not using the term "dream job" to describe a fantasy job that you don't have the skills or temperament for; for example, you dream of being a trauma surgeon but you can't stand the sight of blood. We're also not talking about unrealistic goals for which you do have some of the needed skills, but it would be nearly impossible to achieve your dream. Even if you excel in basketball, it's very unlikely that you could sign with an NBA team when you've only completed the ninth grade—that's something no basketball player has yet achieved.

A dream job is one that you *can get*—it may just take you a few years and some hard work. By planning, getting the right education or training, making contacts in the field, and with some luck, you can land your dream job—or get really close (which means the next job or two might be the "*Bingo!*").

Steps to Your Dream Job

Let's go through the steps—some of which you read about in earlier sections—that will help you land the job of your dreams.

Step 1: Conduct Information Interviews

Too many people make their job hunt harder by starting in the wrong place: they first try to get hiring interviews before they know their best skills, much about the job market, what jobs they want, or how to present themselves. If you don't know three to five jobs in the local labor market that you could do with your skills and the different businesses or sectors of the marketplace (private for-profit, small business, private or public nonprofit) that might have those

WHY DO INFORMATION INTERVIEWS?

Information interviews help you find and then get your dream job. Here are the five top reasons for doing information interviews when you're actively seeking a job—and can immediately take advantage of what you gain from them:

1. You confirm that a certain job is the one you want. An actual job can be quite different from a written job description.

2. Information interviews take the terror out of hiring interviews because you learn how to talk with a professional about the job you're interested in. (Counselors report that it takes teenagers approximately nine information interviews to become comfortable talking with adults about work.)

3. You learn what parts of your experience, training, and education make you a strong job candidate. Knowing that, you can talk about yourself in a hiring interview in a way that will convince your interviewer that you're the right person for the job.

4. Doing information interviews lets an employer see that you're willing to take initiative and responsibility. Both traits are highly valued by employers. (Because of your initiative—as well as your skills and interests—you may find yourself being considered for a job that wasn't even advertised.)

5. Information interviewing can provide you with knowledge—such as job jargon or industry issues—that offsets your lack of work experience.

jobs, you greatly limit your options and set yourself up to get very discouraged. Information interviews help you expand your options through research.

You've already done the exercises in part 1 and identified either three potential dream jobs or three areas of interest, you've made sure these jobs or fields still interest you, and you've reviewed and updated your parachute. You're ready to look for your first full-time job! The first step is to do lots of information interviews. Career coaches estimate it can take over fifty information interviews to find a job that will suit you well. In hard times, you may need as many as two hundred contacts before you get hired. You learned the basics of interviewing for information in chapter 4 and the fundamentals of networking in chapter 8. Now you'll build on those basics.

Remember, information interviewing shouldn't be complicated or intimidating. As we've said before, it's just a conversation with another person about a shared interest or enthusiasm—in this case, a particular job or career. You ask questions, but you'll spend most of your time listening. Let the people you're interviewing tell you their stories about how they came to do the work that interests you. Soon you'll know

- More about the industry or field in which this job happens.

- Common salaries for this work.

- Whether this is a good career choice for you.

- Employers who hire people to do this work.

- Ideas for how you can train for or get such a job.

Information interviews will reveal whether or not your best skills match the most common activities or tasks done in a particular job and how much the work overlaps your interests. Before you ask people to talk with you, read several descriptions of that job, field, industry, or career. You will ask better questions and be a better listener, and the information you collect will make more sense. For each person with whom you have an information interview, use Google or LinkedIn to see what you can learn about them. What you read about an interviewee's background, experience, education, or current position will help focus your questions. Also, your interviewee will be impressed (maybe even flattered) that you took the time to research them.

In this first step, find and talk to people who have jobs or careers that interest you. (These interviews are in *addition* to ones you may have done earlier, in high school, when you were just beginning to research jobs and careers.) If you've targeted three to five potential dream jobs, continue your research by talking with people who do the job you want to do or who work in the same field for each of your dream jobs. Talking with people gives you a reality check for what you've read about a job or your occupational preferences. These conversations

BASIC INFORMATION INTERVIEW QUESTIONS

1. What do you do? What are three to five of the most common tasks or activities you do each day? What skills do you use doing those tasks? Do you mind the repetition?
2. How long have you been doing this work?
3. How did you get into this work?
4. What kind of training or education did you need for this job? How much did it cost?
5. What do you like about your job? What don't you like about your job?
6. What are the main challenges in this industry?
7. What do you see happening in this field in the next five to ten years?
8. What is your ultimate career goal?
9. What is the starting salary in this job or field? What is the salary range with three to six years experience?
10. Do you have any additional comments, suggestions, or advice?
11. Can you give me the names of two or three other people who do this same work?

will help you determine how well each target matches your parachute. The job that matches best will become your #1 job target, the job that matches next best becomes your #2 job target, and so on. Try to find at least three kinds of jobs or careers that overlap with your parachute.

Let's say you're interested in becoming a writer (of articles, books, columns, etc.). You would arrange to interview someone working in that field. Anya's profile (below) is an example of what you might learn in your information interview. You will find additional profiles—of a social media specialist, solar energy sales coordinator, organic farm manager, hazardous waste management specialist, career adviser, and information technology manager—in appendix C. These profiles show you how much important information you can glean from an information interview. They introduce you to different jobs and different types of people. The jobs cover a range of education and training requirements and

WRITER

Name: Anya Kamenetz   **Age:** 29
Job Title: Staff writer for a magazine, author, blogger, speaker
Field: Journalism
Employer(s): *Fast Company* magazine, and myself!
Degree: BA, Yale University
Cost: $120,000
Training: None
Salary: Starting: $12,000 (freelancing), $37,000 (salary); three to six years' experience: $100,000

What do you do?
Using storytelling and other creative techniques, I try to present enlightening, useful, and important ideas in a compelling way in different media: print, online, blog, tweet, audio, video, or in person.

What are the tasks you do most often?
Research by reading things on the Internet. Call people for more information, pitch ideas for stories, and write stories. Concretely, I generally produce anywhere from 5,000 to 10,000 published words in a month, whether that's a book chapter, a long feature story, or many smaller stories or columns. Plus blog and twitter posts. I do about two media interviews a month for radio stations, TV shows, print stories or podcasts, and usually one or two speaking engagements, like a speech at a college or a panel discussion at a conference. I also travel to do on-the-scene reporting for stories.

Do you supervise anyone?
No, thank goodness!

How long have you been at this job?
Since graduating in 2002. I published my first book, *Generation Debt*, in 2006. I was a freelancer/contract worker until January 2008, when I was hired at Fast Company.

How did you get into this work?
My parents are both writers (father, poet and nonfiction; mom, primarily fiction) and I always loved reading and writing. Starting in high school, I developed a bit of a social conscience and decided to combine my love of the craft of writing with the ideal of making a difference in the world. Hence, journalism. Specifically, my dream was to be a staff writer at the *New Yorker*.

continued on next page

PROFILE

continued from previous page

What do you like about your work?

I love my work. I feel incredibly lucky to have work that is creative, engaged with the major issues our society is facing, highly varied, and where I feel like I have a unique contribution to make. In the last few years it has paid more than I ever expected to be making, but I would happily work for less if the job fulfilled more of the above goals or was more flexible.

What don't you like about your job?

Sometimes, I get tired of dealing with PR (public relations) people.

What are the main challenges in this industry?

If you believe the news, this industry is one of the most challenged in our economy, second only to U.S. automaking. Revenue models and mediums are changing fast and I worry about support for quality independent investigative journalism. But I believe fiercely that storytelling and information "curation" will remain valued into the foreseeable future.

What do you see happening in this field in the next 5 to 10 years?

Printers will become empty warehouses. Only a few favored newspapers and magazines will remain on paper as quality heritage designed and printed objects (the *Sunday Times*? *Vogue*? the *New Yorker*?). Television will escape the convention of the daily broadcast schedule to become ubiquitous video-on-demand. New configurations of blogs, microblogs, portals, channels, podcasts, and networks will replace discrete collections of programs and articles. Product placement/integration and psycho-demographic targeting will further blur the lines between display ads and content.

Have you used social networking in a job search?

More accurate to say . . . I have used social networking instead of job searching, as new opportunities find me all the time via Facebook, Twitter, my university's alumni network, and my blog. I have never done a conventional job search.

What is your ultimate career goal?

Keep writing books (the latest, *DIY U*, is about the future of higher education) and build a lifelong career as an internationally known and influential public intellectual (an amalgamation of Malcolm Gladwell + Naomi Klein), while preserving plenty of time for my family and personal life. I would also take staff writer at the *New Yorker*!

Outside your job, what are your other interests or hobbies?

Number one is cooking dinner for my amazing husband—we've been together for ten years, married for three. Yoga, running, novels, movies, spiritual Jewish practice, creative activities with friends, and dancing are all things I might be doing on a good weekend.

Did you have an internship in school? If yes, was it helpful to your employment?

Absolutely. I did my first internship when I was fifteen at a small, free arts magazine in New Orleans, my hometown. I continued breaking into the business through internships in college at *McCall's*, *More* magazine, and finally the *Village Voice*, which became my first real professional home.

What advice would you give a young adult who wants to work in your field?

Be extremely flexible and adaptable because this field is changing fast and no one can tell you exactly what path to follow. Skip grad school. Embrace technology—we can't afford to be humanities snobs. If you're in the media you have to love new media, so find your inner geek.

NOTE: You can find Anya's articles at **www.fastcompany.com** or read her tweets at Twitter: @ANYA1ANYA.

represent a range of salaries. Some of these people feel they have a dream job. Others feel they have a good job. All those profiled enjoy their work.

When you ask the same questions in each interview, you get very different information, and seeing these differences can be very helpful. Notice that the interview questions in this chapter include the ones from chapter 4, but go into more depth and will help you get a better idea of whether or not a job is a good fit for you. Asking these questions takes about a half hour. Make an appointment with your interviewees for thirty minutes. You may want to send them your list of questions ahead of time so they can think about their possible answers. You can ask additional questions, but keep to your time schedule. If you get to the end

> ### DON'T FORGET THE THANK-YOU NOTE
>
> Never underestimate the value of thanking someone for taking time to meet with you. (To review the basics of writing thank-you notes, see page 50.)

of a half hour and still have a couple of questions, ask your interviewee for five or ten more minutes so you can get through your list. After you've done five information interviews for each of the jobs that interest you, you'll be ready for step 2.

Step 2: Cultivate Contacts and Create Networks

The people you meet through information interviewing become contacts and part of your career network. You have a personal network—friends, family, and other people you know—and a professional or work network—people whose work is the same as or similar to what you're interested in doing. Both networks can be helpful in your job search. Keep in touch with your contacts. Send them an update about your life or career at least once a year. Show interest in their lives as well. If you haven't talked with someone for years and suddenly get in touch for help with your job search, they'll feel used—although if they really like you, they may help you anyway. Just as preventative maintenance keeps your car running well, treating your contacts well keeps your networks healthy.

Here's an example of how contacts and networks work. One of your parents' friends (personal network) suggests that you talk to a local banker—not because you want to be a banker, but because bankers know a great deal about various businesses in your area. You have a good conversation with the banker, learn what you want to know (and perhaps a great deal more), and send her a thank-you note after the information interview. Some time later, you want to talk with someone in the construction industry because you're interested in becoming a commercial building contractor. A natural place to start would be with this banker, who is now a contact of yours (professional network). If she doesn't personally know a building contractor with whom you can talk, she's likely to know someone who can make that connection for you.

Contacts become your extra eyes and ears. They may hear about job openings before they become public and alert you to those opportunities. They can help you with specific information you may need—for example, when you want to do an information interview and can't find someone who does exactly the type of work you're looking for. Later, when there's a job you're particularly interested in, they could help you learn the name of the hiring manager or get an appointment with that person. Or, if the job is at the same place where your contact works, he or she may be willing to introduce you to the hiring manager or act as a reference for you. Because employers highly regard the recommendations of their colleagues and employees as to whom they should hire, creating a network of people who do what you want to do more than repays your investment of time and effort.

It's important to keep the contact information of people you meet—names, phone numbers, and addresses (both email and snail mail)—so that you can contact them in the future. Keep this information in your career portfolio (see chapter 5).

You can also get names of people to contact from

- Teachers, relatives, former bosses, and coworkers

- People with whom you've had information interviews

- Members of community service organizations (such as the Lions Club, Kiwanis, Rotary, Soroptimists, Association of University Women, and Boys and Girls Clubs)

- Printed material: the business section of your daily paper or its archives, a company website, Internet research, annual reports or public relations articles compiled by companies themselves

- People you've met through temporary or volunteer work

- Your social networking contacts (by sending out a request through a social networking site or a Twitter post)

We'll return to your contacts and networks a little bit later in this chapter when we look at how to begin your campaign to get hired for a particular job (see page 121).

Step 3: Research Organizations of Interest

Now that you've done your information interviews and prioritized your job targets (step 1), and started cultivating contacts and creating networks (step 2), it's time to find out exactly which organizations hire people to do the job you want to do. Often you can do the same work in several different organizations or businesses. Your information interviews, along with other research, will help you select the places you most want to work.

Building on your information interviews, you will now research more thoroughly the organizations that are likely to offer the job you want. In addition to doing a general Internet search, you can research an organization in many ways; for example:

- Look through the archives of newspapers or periodicals and find written information on the organizations.

- Visit company websites and websites for that field or industry.

- Talk to people who work for (or used to work for) organizations you're interested in. Also, talk with competitors (if this is a business) or people at similar agencies (if this is, for example, a nonprofit agency).

- Talk to the suppliers or customers of a business or a particular department of a corporation.

- Ask for information from business leaders in your community, the local chamber of commerce or private industry council, or the state employment office.

BUT I DON'T HAVE ANY CONTACTS . . .

You probably have more contacts than you realize. Here are a few:

- Family—immediate and extended
- Friends and parents of friends
- Everyone you've friended on Facebook or similar sites
- Neighbors
- Coworkers and employers (past and present)
- School guidance counselors or club sponsors

- Teachers or professors
- Your pastor, rabbi, mullah, youth group leader, or other members of your spiritual community
- People you meet in line at the movies, grocery store, or on vacation
- Mentors or people you've job-shadowed
- Supervisors of your volunteer work or school projects

When you contact people who work for an organization, or used to work for it, you'll want to get answers to the following questions (some of which are difficult to ask directly, so be tactful):

- What kind of work do they do there?

- What kind of goals are they trying to achieve? Are they achieving their goals? (Many organizations have mission statements. Find out which of the organizations that interest you do, and read them.)

- What are their needs, problems, and challenges?

- What obstacles are they running into?

- What kind of reputation does the company have within their industry?

- How do they treat their employees?

Also try to find out how your skills and knowledge can help organizations at which you want to work. People you interview can give you suggestions. When you eventually have hiring interviews, you want to be able to show that you have something to offer—something that they need.

I wish I would have asked more questions about the future of architecture before I decided to become an architect. If I had asked older architects what changes they saw happening to the field, I think I could have anticipated some of the frustrations I'm now having with my profession.

—Award-winning architect
SCOTT J. SMABY

The resources and resource people that you found as you answered all of these questions will give you concrete information about potential places of employment as well as a feel for the work environment at each organization you research. Look at organizations in different sectors of the economy— for-profit or nonprofit (also called nongovernmental organizations, or NGOs). Most likely, some places will be more appealing to you—and probably a better fit for you—than others. That's exactly what you want to find out.

From your research, try to come up with at least five to ten organizations that are potential employers for you. After you've completed your research on various organizations, you will know which ones hire people to do the work you most want to do and which have a work environment that fits you best.

Step 4: Begin Your Campaign to Get the Job You Want

Of the organizations you researched in step 3, choose the top five places you want to work and begin your campaign to get hired. At each of those places, identify the person who has the power to hire you. (This may be the boss in a smaller organization or business, or the hiring manager or a department head in a larger organization.) If you know the name of the person who has the power to hire you, make an appointment. Ask for twenty minutes of his or her time. In asking for an appointment, you can be very direct. Tell this person that you want to discuss the possibility of working for him or her, or with this particular organization or business.

Before your appointment, make an outline of everything you've learned in your information interviewing and your research about this job and company or organization. Be ready to talk about how your skills, training, education, experience, and enthusiasm for this work will make you an outstanding employee.

If there's a company you want to work for and you haven't learned the name of the person who has the power to hire, use your networks—your personal and professional contacts. (Your professional contacts include the people with whom you've done information interviews.) Ask your contacts these questions:

- Do you know someone who works where I want to work?

- Can you give me the name of the person who hires for the job I want?

If you can't get an appointment just by calling and asking for one, again, your network may be able to help. Ask your contacts these questions:

- Do you know the person I want to see?

- Do you know someone who knows the person I want to see?

GOING ONLINE?

Professional chat rooms and message boards are a great way to network online. See if you can find people to answer questions about jobs or careers that interest you at groups.google.com. Whenever you use the Internet, be sure to observe these basic safety rules:

- Never give out your full name, home address, or phone number.
- If anyone writes anything that creeps you out, cease correspondence and tell an adult you trust about it.

Ask whether your contacts can either arrange an introduction for you or call the person you want to meet and recommend that he or she meet with you.

If no offers of employment come from these first five organizations, select five more that have the jobs you want. Keep researching organizations, talking with and expanding the number of people in your network, and asking for interviews until you receive a job offer. Some smart people keep job hunting even if they've gotten a job offer. Sometimes they find an even better opportunity.

While you're taking initiative by contacting organizations you'd like to work for, also watch job listings in the newspaper and online. Once you know which organization or business you want to work for, check their website regularly for job listings. If they don't have a website, call their human resources department to find out how you can learn about job openings. Let both your personal and professional networks know that you're looking for work and what type of work you're seeking. The more approaches you use (up to four from the list on the opposite page) to find your dream job—and the more people who know just what you're looking for—the more likely you'll get that job sooner rather than later.

PARACHUTE TIP

It is not easier to get a job you won't like than one you will. Two simple facts make this true:

1. You will think of all sorts of excuses not to go hunting for a job that doesn't interest you.
2. You will be in competition with people who think this job—the one you don't want—is a dream job. Their enthusiasm will impress an employer. Your lack of enthusiasm will not.

Job-Search Basics

Now that you know the four steps to searching for and finding the job you want, let's take a closer look at some of the basics that will support and guide you as you take each of those steps.

What You Need for Your Job Search

You need to be able to do your job search efficiently in order to be successful. Here are some things you'll need to do that:

- A desk or table. If not available where you live, a library or coffee house will do.

- Some way of storing, organizing, and retrieving information—online or in a notebook—about yourself, employers, and people you've contacted.

- A secure and reliable way of getting phone messages from employers and other contacts. If you don't have voice mail, invest in it for the length of your job search. Your voice mail may be an employer's first impression of you—make it a good one. Your recorded greeting should be businesslike. Clearly state your first and last name. You may also want to mention your job search in your outgoing message. Here's a sample message:

Hi, this is Jessica Wong. I'm sorry I can't take your call right now. Please leave me a message after the beep. I'm currently looking for work in accounting at a hospital or large medical office. If you know of any leads or contacts for me, be sure to mention that too, along with your phone number. Thanks a lot.

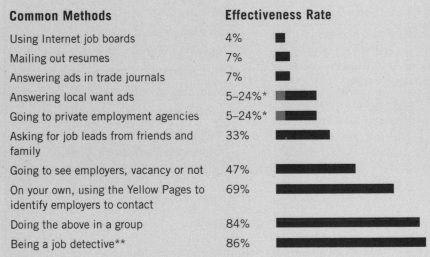

THE BEST WAYS TO LOOK FOR A JOB

Common Methods	Effectiveness Rate	
Using Internet job boards	4%	
Mailing out resumes	7%	
Answering ads in trade journals	7%	
Answering local want ads	5–24%*	
Going to private employment agencies	5–24%*	
Asking for job leads from friends and family	33%	
Going to see employers, vacancy or not	47%	
On your own, using the Yellow Pages to identify employers to contact	69%	
Doing the above in a group	84%	
Being a job detective**	86%	

*The range is due to the level of salary being sought. The higher the salary being sought, the fewer the job hunters who are able to find a job using only this search method.

**A "job detective" follows the strategies used in this book: doing research on oneself, finding jobs that match one's skills and interests, identifying which places of employment have those jobs, and then determining who has the power to hire new staff. We are indebted to Parachute trainer Brian McIvor for this concept, explained in his book *Career Detection: Finding and Managing Your Career* (Management Briefs, 2009). The success rate of the job detective method is twelve times higher than just sending out resumes!

Record your message indoors with no background noise (such as barking dogs or loud music). Speak slowly. Call in and listen to your recording to make sure it can be heard and understood.

- An email address that you can check at least daily. Google, Hotmail, and Yahoo! offer free email. Create a businesslike email address. Again, the first initial of your first name with your last name works well. (Many public libraries provide access to the Internet and email for people who don't have a computer.)

- A professional online Web presence, such as a profile on LinkedIn, where you can post your resume, list your accomplishments, gather recommendations, and so on.

- Reliable transportation, for both interviews and getting to work once you are hired.

- Appropriate interview clothes. Look at how people are dressed at places where you want to work. Wear clothing just a bit more formal than what these workers wear when you go for an information or hiring interview. If you don't have some sharp outfits for interviews, some communities have organizations that help you find good interview clothes for free or low cost.

How To Have a Successful Job Search

Once you have what you need for your job search, the following techniques and suggestions will help you make that search successful.

SEARCH FULL-TIME

If you're out of school, treat your job search as full-time employment. Spend six hours a day, at least four days a week on your job search. You may wonder, "What could possibly keep me busy six hours a day?" To start with, you could spend those hours filling in your parachute and doing the four steps to a dream job over and over until you get hired. The more time you spend actively looking for a job, the quicker your job hunt will go. The average job hunter spends only about five hours a week on searching for a job and sees only two employers a week. It's no surprise, then, that the average job search lasts about seven months.

PROTECT YOUR JOB-SEARCH TIME

Don't let people impose on your job-search time. If you're currently unemployed, your family and friends may be tempted to ask you to do chores or errands. Tell them you'll be glad to help after you finish your job-search activities for the day. Let them know this will be after 3 p.m. If they see that you're serious about devoting at least six hours a day to your job search, they should begin to honor the time you commit to finding the job that's right for you. (And maybe you'll inspire them to find the job that's right for them too!)

MANY VACANCIES AREN'T ADVERTISED

Remember that most vacancies aren't advertised anywhere. Research indicates that 75 to 80 percent of open positions are not listed or published. By doing information interviewing and letting people know what type of position you're looking for, you are likely to find those unadvertised jobs. Of course, you should apply for any advertised vacancy that's of interest to you. Doing that in addition to continuing with your information interviews and keeping in touch with your network of personal and professional contacts will increase your odds of success.

MAKE LOTS OF PHONE CALLS

When you are in step 4, actively trying to get hired, make at least twenty phone calls every morning. Make calls until you've lined up at least two employers who will meet with you each day of the week.

THE ROLE OF LUCK

What is sometimes called "pure dumb luck"—which means having your name in the right place at the right time—plays a crucial role in finding most jobs. But that kind of luck isn't really luck at all but rather the result of good research and savvy networking. The more you meet and talk with people doing the work that you want to do, and the more you keep your professional and personal networks informed about what you're looking for, the more likely you are to get "lucky." For more about the role of luck in your job search, read John Krumboltz and Al Levin's book, *Luck Is No Accident: Making the Most of Happenstance in Your Life and Career* (Impact Publications, 2004).

Who do you call? Start with the employers where you most want to work. If no offers come, use the Yellow Pages of your local telephone directory (or a directory from the area where you want to work). Call businesses, companies, agencies, or organizations likely to employ people who do the work you want. Ask for the manager who hires for the job you want.

What do you say? Create a twenty- to thirty-second pitch. State your name, the work you seek, two or three of your best skills, any machinery or equipment you can operate, or the computer programs you know. Have additional relevant information about your ability to do the job and your prior work experience that you can add in ten- to twenty-second intervals when appropriate in a conversation. You can add the name of your former employer if you have one and you think it will make a good impression.

What do you want? Ask for a fifteen-minute appointment to talk further about your potential as an employee. If somebody will see you, go and sell yourself! If there aren't any openings but somebody will see you anyway, go. Use the time to learn more about the business and the state of the industry, as well as to gain practice selling yourself. If there aren't any vacancies and the person doesn't want to see you, ask whether he or she knows someone who might be interested in your skills. Half the people who use this method get hired in four weeks, and 85 percent have a job in ten weeks.

PRACTICE YOUR PITCH

Write out your pitch and practice it until you can say it slowly and smoothly. Have two or more people listen to it and tell you what they think. Will your pitch get employers interested in seeing you? Here's a good example:

My name is Shannon O'Neal. I'm looking for warehouse work. I'm very good at driving a forklift, entering shipments into computer programs, and tracking them. I can also receive shipments and figure out how to store them so that they can be easily retrieved in the future. My specialty is preparing shipments so that the driver can make deliveries in an organized and logical manner. I'd like to come in and talk with you about my value as an employee.

TARGET SMALL ORGANIZATIONS

Although we hear about large corporations a lot, it's actually small businesses that employ the majority (75 percent) of U.S. workers. Begin your job search with organizations that have twenty-five employees or less. If the work you want to do isn't available at such a small company, find the smallest company at which it is.

It's usually easier to find people who hire for small organizations and easier to get in to see them. Also, small companies can often make faster hiring decisions. Although small businesses prefer to hire people with experience, sometimes their budget doesn't go past entry level. This can work in your favor.

BE PREPARED TO GIVE REFERENCES

If you're looking for a job for the first time, find three or four adults who aren't relatives who are willing to give you positive references. Employers want to know about your reliability and personality. Have you volunteered at your church or for another nonprofit group? Do you belong to a club or community group? Is there a teacher you like or one in whose class you have worked particularly hard? All of these people have seen you at work (even if it hasn't been paid work) and can comment on their knowledge of you as a student or volunteer worker.

Talk to the people who might provide references for you. Tell them that you're looking for your first paying job, and ask them whether they feel they know you or have seen enough of your efforts to give a positive reference. Some will be willing to write you a reference. Others may prefer to give a reference by phone. Try to get at least two or three lined up so that you can provide references quickly if you're asked to do so.

If you have no work or volunteer experience, join a group that interests you. Don't just participate; volunteer to help put together events or meetings. Get to know the group's leaders well enough that they will have a positive opinion of you.

CONSIDER VOLUNTEER WORK

You can do volunteer work while you search for a job, gaining valuable work experience and references in the process. At school, you could volunteer for a leadership program or club. Teachers may be looking for a student assistant; a peer-advising project or tutoring program may need student volunteers. In your community, you might offer to help with child care at your church, volunteer at a nonprofit, or even find a local business that would be willing to let you volunteer. You can volunteer

HOW TO HAVE A SUCCESSFUL JOB SEARCH

- Search full-time.
- Protect your job-search time.
- Remember, many vacancies aren't advertised.
- Make lots of phone calls.
- Practice your pitch.
- Target small organizations.
- Be prepared to give references.
- Consider volunteer work.
- Don't count on resumes to get you a job.
- Take care of yourself.

to be an extra pair of hands or to use and improve your job skills. See whether the organization or agency for which you want to work uses volunteers. If it does, find out how you can do a volunteer internship there. This is a great way to check out an organization from the inside—and also to get references from people in the organization itself. To let your supervisor get to know you, plan on volunteering at least once a week for six to eight weeks.

In the difficult economic conditions that continue as this edition goes to press, knowing how to get the best job you can in any job market is a survival skill. Learn how to do this in good times and bad. Sometimes, pursuing your dream job must take a back seat to pursuing a paycheck. Look at jobs that interest you in some way, even though they're mainly for a paycheck or "just for now." You'll be able to sell yourself better because you like the work.

WHAT—NOTHING ABOUT RESUMES?

You may be starting to wonder why we haven't talked about resumes. This book doesn't include anything on resumes for several reasons:

- There are many other places to get help writing a resume (career centers, resume books, career websites).

- Resumes are not a very effective job-search tool, and they're even less effective for younger workers who don't have a great deal of experience in the jobs or fields in which they most want to work.

- Many people depend too much on a resume to get them a job. It's more important to identify your best skills and interests.

- You can do information interviews without a resume. In fact, you'll be able to write a better resume after you do information interviews.

If you want to learn more about how and when to use resumes in your job search, check out *Don't Send a Resume: And Other Contrarian Rules to Help Land a Great Job* by Jeffrey J. Fox (Hyperion, 2001) and Tom Jackson's classic, *The Perfect Resume* (Broadway, 2004).

TAKE CARE OF YOURSELF

A job hunt can be very rewarding, but rarely is it easy. It demands physical, mental, and emotional energy. It's important to remember that searching for a job is like anything else—it takes time to do it well, so be gentle with yourself in the job-search process.

Because it's so demanding, a job search can wear down the confidence of even the most positive person. To deal with this, we suggest that you don't focus on whether or not you've gotten the job you want. Instead, keep track of how many phone calls, information interviews, hiring interviews, or new contacts you make each day. These numbers mean that you're conducting

an effective job search. You also may want to consider creating an "advisory board" for your job search. Arrange to meet once a month with people who are very good at getting jobs they like (perhaps someone you met while doing information interviews), people who know a lot about the industry or field you want to work in, or people who are supportive even when things are challenging. Ask two or three people whether you can meet with them once a month to get their advice, suggestions, or simply their support during your job search.

Be sure you take care of your physical needs too. Eat right, get enough sleep, drink eight glasses of water a day, and avoid negative people, as this can negatively affect how you look and your energy level. Exercise four or five days a week, listen to motivational tapes, see good friends, and watch movies that make you laugh or give you hope. If there are other things you enjoy doing that help you take care of yourself, be sure to incorporate them into your off (job-search) time.

Tips for the Hiring Interview

Hiring interviews can be stressful. They've often been compared to blind dates, because people applying for jobs often go on interviews without knowing anything about their "date" (the interviewers and the company, organization, or agency where they're interviewing). The more prepared you are, the better your interviews will go. Think about the following scenario:

You are an employer. You are interviewing two applicants for one job. The first seems either scared or bored, you aren't sure which. Her answers are brief. When asked why she wants the job, she replies that the pay is good and it's an easy commute. The other applicant begins by thanking you for the interview, then tells you about the classes she has taken to prepare for this work and the internships she's done to help her hone her on-the-job skills. When asked why

Take a trip to the company or business before your actual interview day. Figure out how long it's likely to take you to get there at the same time of day as your interview. Learn where to park, what bus to take, where the building entrance is, and so on. If you do this before the interview, you'll be less stressed the day of the interview. The less stressed-out you are, the more confident you'll seem.

she wants the job, this applicant tells you that she wants to work for your company because of its great reputation and hopes you'll hire her. But if you don't, she is going to keep applying for jobs like this because it's what she loves to do and believes she is meant to do.

Which applicant would you hire? Commitment, appropriate qualifications, and enthusiasm will make you an outstanding candidate. So learn as much as you can about the job you want, the company you want to work for, and which of your skills make you a good candidate for the job. Also study the following tips for before, during, and after the interview. They'll help you make a great impression.

Before Your Interview

Interviewing isn't that hard. It's a matter of knowing how to talk to someone in a focused manner. The more homework you've done about yourself, the job you want, and the organization where you have an interview, the better the interview is likely to go.

Before your interview, think about these two basic questions:

1. What do I still need to know about this job at this organization?

2. What information do I need to communicate about myself?

To prepare yourself for your interview, practice answering typical interview questions. (See the resources section at the end of this chapter for books and other sources on possible interview questions.) It's helpful to remember that all interview questions are variations on the following questions:

• Why are you here?

• What can you do for us?

• Can I afford you?

• What kind of a person are you? Do I want you working for me?

- What distinguishes you from nineteen other people who can do the same tasks that you can?

You can think of these as the questions behind the actual questions you'll be asked. No matter how a question is phrased, if you know what's *really* being asked, you can choose the best information about yourself to answer the question. Select examples from your experience to show that you've used the skills the job needs or to show that you pick up new skills quickly. Let's say you're interviewing for a job as a receptionist at a medical office. If you're asked, "What can you do for us?" tell your interviewer that you've had experience answering phones and taking messages at the insurance office where you worked part-time in high school. As a candy striper, you learned a lot of medical terminology, as well as how to work with people who are ill.

THINGS TO AVOID IN AN INTERVIEW

- Arriving late
- Bad personal hygiene
- Excess cologne
- Inappropriate clothing
- Lack of initial eye contact
- Mispronouncing your interviewer's name
- Rudeness of any sort
- A weak handshake
- Keeping your iPod or MP3 player hung around your neck
- Not turning off your cell phone

Job-search experts report that it takes people about seven interviews to feel comfortable enough to interview well. That's a good reason to do lots of practice interviews before you proceed with the real ones. Ask adults or friends you trust to put you through mock interviews and check out your handshake—it shouldn't be too strong or too weak. This kind of practice will help you get better at knowing what to say and how to talk, remembering to breathe and thinking clearly even when you're stressed.

During Your Interview

Personnel professionals tell us that many interviewers make up their mind about you in the first half-minute of the interview. They spend the remaining time looking for reasons to justify their decision. Here are the three factors that most often influence your interviewer's first impression of you:

1. Were you on time for the interview?

2. Did you look the interviewer in the eye as you greeted him or her?

3. What was the quality of your handshake?

Interviewers also assess your attitude. They are likely to notice right away whether you are

- A pleasant person to be around—or not

- Interested in other people—or totally absorbed with yourself

- At peace with yourself and the world—or seething with anger beneath a calm exterior

- Outgoing or introverted

- Communicative or monosyllabic

- Focused on giving—or only on taking

- Anxious to do the best job possible—or just going through the motions

WHAT INTERVIEWERS NOTICE

A detailed study done by Albert Merhabian, PhD, at UCLA a couple of years ago revealed some surprising things about what interviewers pay attention to. It turns out that interviewers are preoccupied with nonverbal communication, to make sure it matches up with what the interviewee is saying (and if it doesn't, they're less likely to hire that applicant!).

Percentage of attention:

Focused on:

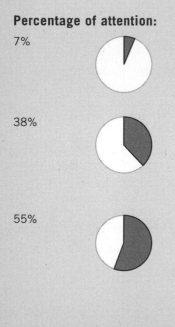

7%

WORDS
Choose your words carefully. In three different ways, explain the skills, experience, or training that most qualify you for this job.

38%

VOICE QUALITY
Don't have too much caffeine before an interview. If your voice tends to get high-pitched when you're nervous, take a thermos of warm water with you and have some sips before your interview starts.

55%

NONVERBAL (handshake, posture, what you do with your hands, nervous mannerisms, eye contact, and so on)
Don't always look your interviewer straight in the eye. This can be seen as threatening. Alternate direct looks with looking past his or her ear, slightly above the head.

They also notice whether you project energy and enthusiasm or expend only a minimal amount of effort and exude a sense of sullenness. In many cases, your attitude is even more important than your skills, because it indicates how hard you're willing to work and whether you can work well with other people. Employers will hire someone with lesser skills but with a good attitude before they'll hire a more experienced and more skilled person with a bad attitude.

Don't expect your interviewer to make a connection between your past experience or what's on your resume and your ability to do this job, even if it's exactly the same work you've done before. You must explain your experience and skills to the interviewer and show that you are qualified to do the job. Young people are often surprised how hard they have to sell themselves in an interview, even if the interviewer knows them.

Your interviewer is also trying to judge how quickly you can become productive if you're hired. The way you conduct yourself in the interview gives a lot of clues as to what type of employee you'll be. Here are a few helpful hints for effective interviews:

- Mix speaking and listening equally so the interview feels like a friendly conversation. People hire people they like. If interviewers don't feel comfortable talking with you, they probably won't like you enough to offer you a job.

- Answer the interviewer's questions. Don't go off on tangents. Vary the length of your answers between twenty seconds and two minutes.

DON'T GET DISCOURAGED

If your faith in finding your dream job is flagging, use your contacts to meet people who have found their dream jobs. Ask them to tell you how they got their job. See whether they can help you adapt what they learned to your job search. Find and read inspiring books or articles on people who love their work. Other people's stories help you stay positive.

Some people get their dream job right away. More people, however, get there in several steps. Each time you have a setback, redouble your efforts to find people doing the work you hope to do—the younger in age, the better. If you work at it, you will get there.

Remember, Anya Kamenetz got her first writing internship at fifteen. After high school, she continued to find internships and get jobs at magazines so she could hone her craft. It took another dozen years before she finally became a successful author and well-paid writer. Reread Anna's profile on page 115.

- Speak well (or not at all) of your previous employer. If your experience with them wasn't that good, think out how you can describe what you did and learned without bad-mouthing them.

Though it may be hard to believe, remember that many interviewers are as scared as you are during the hiring interview. They don't want to make a hiring mistake. It's definitely to your advantage to help make the interviewer feel comfortable. Sometimes it's helpful to remember that you are interviewing the interviewer as much as the interviewer is interviewing you. Through your questions, you'll get information that will help you determine whether this is the right job and the right place for you.

In an interview, you're judged just as much on the questions you ask as on those you answer. The questions you ask reveal how much you know about the work, the industry or field, and the organization. Here are two important questions to ask your interviewer.

1. *What does this job involve?* You want to understand exactly what tasks will be asked of you so that you can determine whether these are the kinds of tasks you really like and want to do. If you have done information interviews of people who do this work, you can let your interviewer know what the job entails in other companies. Even if you've done excellent research on this job and employer, you may find that the interviewer has additional or different ideas about what the job will involve. You need to know what those expectations are. If you know your interviewer's expectations, you can better pick what skills or experiences you use to show your interviewer that you can do the job and meet their expectations.

2. *What are the skills a top employee in this job needs to have?* You want to know whether your skills match those that the employer wants a top employee to have. Which of your skills match those of a top employee? Be able to state these skills and give examples of how you've used them in similar situations.

As we just pointed out, you're interviewing the interviewer or employer too. Be sure to ask these three questions of *yourself* (not the interviewer):

1. *Do I want to work with these people?* Pay attention to your intuition. Sometimes your interviewer will give all the "right" answers to your questions, but you'll still have an uneasy feeling. Don't ignore that feeling. You want to know whether you can work well with these people and whether

they share values that are important to you. You want a work environment where you'll thrive. Author and venture capitalist Guy Kawasaki put it starkly: "In a job, your real job is to make your boss look good." During an interview, ask yourself, "Is this person someone I want to work hard for and make him or her look good?"

2. *Can I do this job? Do I want to do this job?* Back in chapter 1, we talked about "can-do" skills and "want-to" skills. Be sure you know which skills you really want to use in a job. You're much more likely to be happy in a job that uses a high number of the skills you want to use.

3. *If the job seems to be a good fit, can I persuade the organization that there's something that makes me different from other people who can do the same tasks?* It's important to formulate an answer to this question before you walk into the interview. You need to know how you work and be able to describe it. What is the style in which you do your work (for example, independently, collaboratively, quickly, carefully, and so on)? Ideally, your style fits with what your hoped-for employer is looking for.

TIPS FOR HIRING INTERVIEWS

Before your interview, ask yourself these questions:

- What information do I need to communicate about myself?
- What do I need to know about this job at this organization?

At your interview:

- Be on time.
- Look the interviewer in the eye as you greet him or her.
- Shake hands warmly and firmly.
- Ask your interviewer these questions:
  - What does this job involve (from the interviewer's perspective)?
  - What are the skills a top employee in the job needs to have?
- Ask yourself these questions:
  - Do I want to work with these people?
  - Can I do this job? Do I want to do this job?
  - Can I persuade the interviewer that there's something that makes me different from other people who can do the same tasks?

After your interview:

- Always send a thank-you note.

Ending an Interview with Finesse

As the interview proceeds, if the interviewer's questions move from the past toward the future, the interview is going well. If you are determined to get a certain job, always ask the following five questions before the end of the interview. Don't be afraid to speak up—you need the answers to these questions.

1. Can you offer me this job? (If you want the job, be sure to ask for it; 20 percent of the people who ask for a job get it.)

2. Do you want me to come back for another interview, perhaps with some of the other decision makers here?

3. When may I expect to hear from you?

4. What is the latest I can expect to hear from you?

5. May I contact you after that date, if for any reason you haven't gotten back to me by that time?

If, however, it's clear from the interview that the interviewer doesn't view you as qualified for this particular job, don't assume all is lost. Be sure to ask these two questions:

1. Do you have work for which you do think I'm qualified?

2. Can you think of anyone else who might be interested in hiring me?

After an Interview

STUCK ON THE THANK-YOU?

You can learn more about writing thank-you notes by doing an Internet search on "job interview thank-you notes."

Always send a thank-you note to your interviewer. If more than one person was involved in the interview, send a thank-you note to each person on the interview team. (To review thank-you note basics, see chapter 4.)

- Thank your interviewer for his or her time.

- If you enjoyed meeting the interviewer, say so.

- Remind the interviewer of one or two parts of your background (skills, training, or previous jobs) that qualify you for the job. When you write your note, don't make it too long.

A letter of just three or four paragraphs (with three to four sentences in each paragraph) can be read quickly. A longer letter may make your interviewer think that you're doing another interview in writing rather than saying thank you. Always make certain your note—whether typed or email—is grammatically correct with no spelling errors. Send it within twenty-four hours of your interview.

You're Hired! Now What?

Congratulations! All your hard work has paid off and you've been hired. Over the next few weeks, let your contacts and professional network know your job hunt has been successful. Enjoy the good news and be sure to celebrate.

Now, of course, you'll start your new job. Is there something else you should be doing? The late John Crystal, author and creative job-search pioneer, once said, "To take charge of your career, you need to look further down the road than headlight range. You need to begin your next job hunt the day you start your current job."

Oof! That's probably not what you wanted to hear right now. But taking charge of your career is simply a continuation of what you've already been doing—from identifying your skills and interests to naming your potential dream jobs, from getting the appropriate training or education to researching and interviewing for this particular job. It may be that the job you've just gotten isn't quite your dream job, but it is a step on the way toward that dream job. To help you continue on the road to your dream job, we have a few more recommendations for you.

Start a Job Journal

Each week, spend ten to fifteen minutes making notes about what you did during the week. (Friday after lunch is a great time to update your job journal.) Jot down names of projects, tasks, activities, or important meetings. Make notes about what should be included in a future job portfolio. Note what you like with a + and use a − for job duties you didn't like. Be sure to include committees you've been asked to serve on and the names of professional organizations you've joined. (Also note any offices you may hold.)

After a couple of months, it's easy to forget what you've done. If you write down all the tasks and responsibilities of your job, you won't forget them. Your job journal will be a valuable resource when you face performance reviews and self-evaluations, as well as when you begin the search for your next job or take the next step toward your dream job.

Identify the Members of the "A Team"

As you become familiar with your new work environment, begin to meet and observe people throughout the organization. Who are the up-and-comers? Is there a manager you would rather work for or a division you would rather work in? Get to know the people who have the jobs you want. Get to know their managers too. Don't go around saying, "I want your job"; you won't build good relations with your colleagues that way. But do ask people about the specifics of their jobs. By doing information interviews at work, you can develop a plan for the next step in your career.

Watch, Listen, and Learn

If you join a business, division, or department that has two or more people, be aware that you're entering a situation that has a history. There are ongoing dynamics and power struggles about which you know nothing yet. As you learn your way around, observe everyone and everything. Don't overdo sharing of personal information or get overly friendly until you know someone's motives. After a few weeks of watching the scene, you'll probably put together what's going on.

Find a Mentor

In fact, find several mentors. If this is a company in which you hope to have a long-term career, find a mentor within the company. (For more on mentors, see chapter 5.) If you like the industry, find one or more mentors outside the company. You can pick people who are still working or who have retired. Choose someone who has achieved the level of success to which you aspire. Meet with your mentors at least twice a year.

This has been a long chapter. That's because there is so much to learn if you want your job hunt to be successful. We hope you've learned a lot about how to search for and find your dream job. In the next chapter, we'll look at the top ten mistakes job-hunters make—and how you can avoid them.

IF YOU WANT TO EXPLORE FURTHER . . .

Job Hunting: General Information

Bermont, Todd. *Get the Job You Want: 10 Secrets to a Winning Job Search.* Troutman, 2009.

Coon, Nora. *Teen Dream Jobs: How to Find the Job You Really Want Now!* Beyond Words Publishing, 2003.

Fox, Jeffrey J. *Don't Send a Resume: And Other Contrarian Rules to Help Land a Great Job.* Hyperion, 2001.

Levinson, Jay. *Guerrilla Marketing for Job Hunters.* Wiley, 2005.

McIvor, Brian. *Career Detection: Finding and Managing Your Career.* Management Briefs, 2009.

Reeves, Ellen. *Can I Wear My Nose Ring to the Interview? A Crash Course in Finding, Landing, and Keeping Your First Real Job.* Workman, 2009.

Vernon, Naomi. *A Teen's Guide to Finding a Job,* 2nd ed. AuthorHouse, 2003.

Webster, Jeanne. *If You Could Be Anything, What Would You Be? A Teen's Guide to Mapping Out the Future.* Dupuis North Publishing, 2004.

Get all kinds of ideas for your search from career strategist Marty Nemko, PhD, at his website: **www.martynemko.com**.

What to expect during your job search: **www.amny.com/urbanite-1.812039/what-to-expect-in-your-job-search-1.1480682**.

This fun site has career advice and job listings for the upper Midwestern states: **www.jobdig.com**.

A site with job listings from around the country and around the world: **www.craigslist.org**.

For links to Internet employment resources, check out **www.jobhunt.com**.

Bob Rosner's site tackles getting and keeping a job in tough times: **http://workplace911.com**.

Job Hunting: Interview Preparation

Beshara, Tony. *Acing the Interview: How to Ask and Answer Questions That Will Get You the Job.* Amacom, 2008.

Gottesman, Deb, and Buzz Mauro. *The Interview Rehearsal Book.* Berkley Trade, 1999.

Kador, John. *201 Best Questions to Ask on Your Interview*. McGraw-Hill, 2002.

McIvor, Brian. *Be Interview Wise: How to Prepare for and Manage Your Interviews*. Management Briefs, 2009.

Porot, Daniel. *Best Answers to 202 Job Interview Questions: Expert Tips to Ace the Interview and Get the Job Offer*. Impact, 2008.

This link will show you some dos and don'ts of dressing for an interview: **http://jobsearch.about.com/od/teenstudentgrad/ig/Interview-Attire/**.

Job Hunting: Special Resources

Bolles, Richard Nelson, and Dale S. Brown. *Job-Hunting for the So-Called Handicapped*. Ten Speed Press, 2001. This book deals with the specific challenges faced by job hunters with disabilities.

Cooper, Barbara. *The Social Success Workbook for Teens: Skill-Building Activities for Teens with Nonverbal Learning Disorder, Asperger's Disorder & Other Social-Skill Problems*, 2nd ed. New Harbinger, 2008.

Kruempelmann, Elizabeth. *The Global Citizen: A Guide to Creating an International Life and Career*. Ten Speed Press, 2002. This is geared toward people who want to work and experience life abroad.

Landes, Michael. *The Back Door Guide to Short-Term Job Adventures*, 4th ed. Ten Speed Press, 2005. This book includes information on internships, seasonal work, volunteer jobs, and adventures abroad.

Career coach Robin Roman Wright works with all young adult job seekers. She's a specialist at dealing with the job-search frustrations of those with ADHD. Contact her at her website: **www.youthleadershipcareers.com**.

Mentoring

This site has general information about mentoring. Enter your zip code to find programs in your area. **www.mentoring.org**

For links to teen mentoring programs around the world, go to **www.yess.co.nz/RobinsGreatLinks.html**.

New Jobs—After You're Hired

Kitson, Michael and Calandra. *How to Keep Your Job in a Tough Competitive Market*. Adams Media, 2009.

Williams, Anna, et al. *The Family Guide to the American Workplace*. Learnovation, 2003. See, in particular, chapters 3 (Beginning Your New Job) and 4 (Learning the Job).

Salary Information

Porot, Daniel. *101 Salary Secrets: How to Negotiate Like a Pro*. Ten Speed Press, 2000.

Canadian readers can check out salaries in their country at **http://swz.salary.com/csalarywizard/layoutscripts/cswzl_newsearch.asp**.

The Riley Guide is a dependable resource for job seekers. You can find salary info at **www.rileyguide.com/salguides.html**.

Some job descriptions give salary information based on national averages. The area where you want to live may have salaries higher or lower than the national norm. To check out salaries by zip code, check out this website: **www.salary.com**.

10

The Top 10 Mistakes Job Hunters Make—and How *You* Can Avoid Them

Along with the job-search strategies and techniques you've learned in the previous chapters, avoiding the mistakes job hunters commonly make will help you win the job-hunting game. Here are the ten most common mistakes and how you can avoid them.

1. Acting As If Someone Owes You a Job

In the job-search process, it's important to remember that no one owes you a job. You have to earn it yourself. Successful job hunters don't act as if an employer owes them a job, but they do make every effort to let the employer know that they would be an excellent employee, thus impressing the employer with their enthusiasm and attitude. If you want a particular job, put all your effort into going after it and use everything that you've learned about yourself and how to be an effective job hunter.

2. Spending Too Little Time on the Job Search

Successful job hunters quickly learn that the amount of success they experience in their job hunt is in direct proportion to the time they spend at it. Two-thirds of all job hunters spend five hours or less a week on their job search. If you are unemployed, you should spend six hours a day at your job search. If you are employed, you'll be amazed at what you can accomplish in twenty minutes a day. Let's say you know it will take you two hundred hours to get a new job. If you put in six hours a day, five days a week, it's quite possible you'll be starting your new job within seven weeks. If you job-hunt one hour a day, five days a week, it will take you forty weeks (ten months) to find a job. Which approach seems best to you?

> What accounts for the difference between greatness and mediocrity? Extraordinary drive.
>
> —BENJAMIN BLOOM

Obviously, it's not possible to know exactly how long it will take you to find a job because the job hunt is full of factors you can't predict or control. If you are spending six hours a day (or twenty minutes if you are employed) and you aren't getting the results you want in your job search, meet with a couple of members of your job search advisory board. Tell them what you've been doing to find a job and ask for their suggestions.

3. Continuing To Use Techniques That Aren't Working

Successful job hunters change tactics when change is needed. When any job-hunting behavior, attitude, or technique doesn't work for you, try something new. (See chapter 9 for specific tactics to use.) For example, if you haven't had any interviews after a month of using a certain technique—say, sending out resumes or answering ads—change your tactics. Start doing more information interviews and spend more time researching organizations that you find interesting.

Expand what you've learned in this book about effective job-search techniques by reading other good job-search books and consulting online resources. (See the resources sections at the end of preceding chapters.) Talk with successful job hunters and ask what worked for them. Find a support group for job hunters. Your local employment office may sponsor one; some churches do, as well.

4. Ignoring What Others Have Learned

People who succeed in job hunting talk with other successful job hunters. As we suggested in the discussion of mistake #3, it's important to talk with people who have succeeded in finding a job they love. Learn from people who are job-hunting masters.

Ask family members, friends, teachers, and others in your personal and professional networks to help you find successful job hunters. Talk to at least four people who have found a job that they like in the last six months. Use every technique that worked for them. If necessary, modify the techniques to fit the job you seek.

Job-search mentors can also be very helpful. You need more than one person's point of view for good perspective, so ask two to four people to mentor you through your job hunt. If you know some people who you think are pretty sharp, ask them whether they'd be willing to meet with you once a month to advise you. Each time you meet, update them on what you've done and ask for their ideas on how to improve.

> I received an email from someone whose most recent job was in microelectronics. He wanted another job in that industry. It took him fourteen hundred inquiries to get the message that the jobs he wanted have almost completely been moved to Asia. If you make ten inquiries and everyone says no one's hiring, expand your geographic boundaries, or change your target field.
>
> —MARTY NEMKO, career coach and author of *Cool Careers for Dummies*

5. Playing at Job Hunting

Successful job hunters treat the job hunt as a job, not as a game. Think of yourself as having a full-time job (without pay) every weekday. By 9 a.m. each weekday, be showered, groomed, and dressed in business casual. If you aren't sure how to dress, visit the places you want to work and see how people are dressed. Then select clothing one notch more formal. If you're dressed for work, you can be out the door quickly if someone says, "I can see you now." Job hunters who have great success at getting hiring interviews report that they spend five to eight hours a day in job-search activities such as creating an overall job-search strategy, reviewing skills and experience relevant to the work desired, identifying job targets, making contacts, reading articles on job-search techniques, doing Internet research, setting up interviews, and writing thank-you notes.

6. Being Financially Unprepared

Successful job hunters assess their financial situation realistically—unsuccessful job hunters don't. Most likely, your job search will last between five and twenty weeks, even if you work at it full-time. Prepare yourself mentally and financially for your job hunt. Assume it will last a lot longer than you think it will. Ask yourself these questions:

- Given the money in my pocket, bank account, savings, piggy bank, or other sources, how long can I afford to live without having a job?

- Can I get help with buying interview clothes or paying for transportation costs, voicemail, and internet access?

- Am I eligible for any assistance from public agencies or nonprofit organizations in my area?

- Am I living at home or can I move back home?

- What support can my parents provide? (Ask how long they're willing to support you while you look for a job. Don't assume their financial support will go on indefinitely.)

- Can I lower my expenses? (Thoroughly assess your financial resources and put the brakes on unnecessary spending.)

- Can I move to a less expensive place?

- Can I earn part of my rent in exchange for doing chores or maintenance?

7. Giving Up Too Easily and Too Soon

Successful job hunters are persistent. Various studies on job hunting indicate that one-third of all job hunters give up during the first two months of their job hunt. They give up because they thought job hunting would be simple, quick, and easy. (In times when the nation's economy isn't doing well, job-search experts estimate that job hunters will make about two hundred contacts before finding a job.)

Many employers eliminate job hunters from consideration for jobs based on their job-search behavior—particularly any lack of initiative and persistence—so keep going until you find a job. Here are some examples of being persistent.

- Sending an email resume, then sending a resume by mail, then following up a few days later with a phone call.

- Being willing to go back to places that interest you to see whether by any chance their "no vacancy" or initial lack of interest in you has changed.

- Asking yourself, "What businesses need someone with my skills or knowledge?" until you find one that wants to hire you.

- Making the fourth, fifth, or sixth phone call to find someone who knows the people who have the power to hire at the places where you want to work.

8. Having Only One Job Target

Successful job hunters have more than one job target. They are well aware that in this rapidly changing world, jobs do vanish. Therefore, use your interests, experience, values, best skills, and whatever else is important to you in a job to identify three or four other lines of work you can do, and would enjoy doing. Never put all your eggs in one basket.

Be open to new possibilities. Don't label yourself so that you think there's only one thing you can do. Don't define yourself in terms of your current or former job title. You are not a fast-food worker, a retail salesperson, or an army vet. Define yourself in terms of the skills you have—what you know and what you can do.

Ironically, defining yourself—and your job hunt—too broadly can be just as detrimental as defining yourself and the job you're looking for too narrowly. Don't tell others you're looking for "anything." Be specific about the jobs you want.

> Nobody in life gets exactly what they thought they were going to get. But if you work really hard and you're kind, amazing things will happen. I'm telling you, amazing things will happen.
>
> —CONAN O'BRIEN

9. Limiting Your Job Search to What's "Out There"

Successful job hunters go after the jobs they want the most, even if those jobs aren't advertised. You can do that too. Remember, you'll be more likely to find something you want if you look for something you want. (Review Steps to Your Dream Job in chapter 9.)

10. Thinking You Must Do This All By Yourself

Successful job hunters ask for help. Once you know what kind of work you're looking for, get out your address book, contact all the people in your Blackberry, send out a tweet, post a notice on your Facebook wall, or send out a message through MySpace. Call everyone you know. Tell them what work you want and ask whether they know someone who does that work. If you know where you want to work, ask them whether they know someone who works at that place. Ask your parents, relatives, friends, friends' parents, teachers, people you know at

PARACHUTE TIP

Find a job-search buddy. Do you (or anyone in your personal or professional network) know of someone who is looking for work? You'll be more persistent, get more support, uncover more leads, and even have more fun if you job-hunt with a friend.

your place of worship, and current or former coworkers for suggestions of other people you might contact. Follow up on every lead you are given.

The most effective—and least used—job-search strategy is to meet at least twelve people who either do exactly the work you want to do or are employed in the same industry. Ask them to notify you if they hear of job openings that fit what you're looking for. These twelve people then become twelve sets of eyes and ears helping you with your job search.

• • •

By avoiding these top ten mistakes, you will become a successful job hunter. When you need a quick review of job-search basics, come back to this list. Knowing what not to do—and even more important, knowing what to do—will put you way ahead of less determined job hunters.

11

Tracking Emerging Career Trends

GREEN CAREERS AND SUSTAINABILITY

Change is happening so fast in the economic marketplace that if you want to keep your career on a certain track, you'll have to keep learning how to develop your career. You'll need to keep your skills sharpened and keep exploring careers, especially those in emerging fields.

Once you are out of school and employed, you can't expect your employer to plan your advancement for you. Your career is under your command. Recruiters and executive coaches suggest that their clients write a new resume each New Year's Day, whether they are job hunting or not. In truth, most people probably spend more time filing their nails than building a strategy to get and keep jobs they like. Although updating your resume at least annually is a good idea, it's not much of a strategy for advancement. Keeping track of the new jobs that interest you and trends emerging in your own field is a much better use of your time. Talking with your mentors and colleagues and attending professional functions are good ways to track industry changes as well. With the rapid change in the skills needed in the workforce, you may find your next career move is into a job that has only just morphed into reality.

One trend is the emergence and growth of "green jobs" and the greening of jobs in general. Green jobs or greening jobs are happening in nearly every type of industry and business. Even in the United States, where expensive consumer items have long been considered disposable, there is a growing awareness of finite resources and the need to conserve them. If, like many, you long to do something good for the world while earning a living, you may find your parachute is green!

Despite what you may have heard, the number of green jobs is still steadily growing. There is an incredible variety of green jobs and careers. Green jobs are found in virtually all industries and career areas. Green jobs are found in all states. Some green jobs reflect new and emerging occupations; others reflect jobs that have been around for decades. Some are green-collar jobs—meaning they are skilled trade jobs that require many skills but don't usually require a college degree. Some may require little or no training. Some others require a master's or doctoral degree. People with all different levels of skills can find green jobs.

WHAT ARE GREEN JOBS?

According to a White House task force, they are jobs that provide products and services that use renewable energy resources, reduce pollution, conserve energy and natural resources, and reconstitute waste.

What fields are associated with green jobs? Here are a few:

- Clean and renewable energy

- Energy efficiency

- Environmental protection and preservation

- Green building and sustainable design

- Organic and recycled (ecofriendly) products

- Sustainable business practices, including clean tech

What types of occupations can lead to green jobs? The majority of green jobs fall into one of seven basic career clusters (pathways):

1. Engineering and mechanical careers

2. Environmental health/safety and regulatory careers

3. Green building, sustainable design, and energy efficiency careers

4. Green business and enterprising careers

5. Natural and land resource management careers

6. Natural sciences and physical geography careers

7. Sustainable and organic agriculture careers

And, jobs that aren't "green" to start with can be greened, if you know how and have an employer willing to let you try.

There is a growing amount of information about green jobs, both in print and on the Web. Some resources are listed at the end of this chapter.

Sustainable Careers

You may be familiar with the words "sustainable" and "sustainability." You will certainly hear them more in the coming years. When we call something sustainable, this means it can easily be maintained and renewed over time. The term is also used to refer to the use of natural resources without depleting them or destroying the ecology. The concept of sustainability has many implications for your work life.

THINK YOU'RE GREEN?

To learn the size of your ecological footprint, take the quiz at: **www.myfootprint.org/en/visitor_ information**.

WHAT IS A SUSTAINABLE ORGANIZATION OR BUSINESS?

There is no standard criteria. To be considered sustainable or green, here are some basic criteria:

- Complies with all environmental regulations

- Conserves energy and water

- Prevents pollution

- Reduces, reuses, and recycles

- Uses renewable energy

- Responsibly measures, controls, and reduces the organization's carbon footprint

To steer your career toward success, you will also want to analyze the natural resources needed by and affected by the kind of work you want to do. Are those resources becoming scarce and more expensive? Just as the once-fashionable tall beaver hats worn by men (think President Lincoln) disappeared because beavers were overhunted, resources that are depleted, becoming overly expensive in the process, cause jobs to dwindle as well. If the materials necessary for your job become harder to get, or are predicted to, begin your quest for a new job.

Financial Sustainability

Remember the definition of sustainable as something that is easily maintained? If your combined student loan and credit card debt exceeds two-thirds of your starting salary, you won't find it easy to maintain yourself.

When you have a job that is financially sustainable, your income covers your bills (and those of your dependents) and allows for saving. As you make decisions about the kind of work you want to do, consider how much the training, internships, or education to qualify for that work will cost you. What would your starting salary be? If the necessary studies will put you in debt for more than the annual salary you'll make starting out, that choice is not financially sustainable. Both a dream job and a good job need to be financially sustainable. This doesn't mean you should give up a career path because it is too expensive to pursue at the moment. You may need to alternate education and work for a number of years until you can afford to study exactly what you want. Remember the preface to this book? If it's going to take you about ten years to become financially independent or assemble the education and experience that your dream job needs, you've got time to climb that education and work ladder.

IF YOU WANT TO EXPLORE FURTHER...

We are heavily indebted to author workforce consultant Jim Cassio for tutoring us about green jobs. You can thank him by buying the book he coauthored with Alice Rush:

Cassio, Jim, and Alice Rush. *Green Careers: Choosing Work for a Sustainable Future* by New Society Publishers, 2009. You can also visit his website, **www.cassio.com**, where you can download his free e-book *Green Careers Resource Guide* or sign up for one of his informative workshops on green careers.

Llewellyn, A. Bronwyn, James P. Hendrix, and K. C. Golden. *Green Jobs: A Guide to Eco-Friendly Employment*. Adams Media, 2008.

Everett, Melissa. *Making a Living While Making a Difference*. New Society Publishers, 2007.

Hunter, Malcolm L. Jr., David Lindenmayer, and Aram Calhoun. *Saving the Earth as a Career: Advice on Becoming a Conservation Professional*. Wiley-Blackwell, 2007.

Green Career Job Boards

Green Career Central **www.greencareercentral.com**

Green Careers Center **www.environmentalcareer.com**

Green Dream Jobs **www.sustainablebusiness.com/jobs/**

Green Careers Networking Sites

www.ecotuesday.com

www.greendrinks.org

www.greenjobs.net

12

Beyond Your Dream Job

CREATING THE LIFE YOU WANT

You've probably heard the saying "There's more to life than work." We agree wholeheartedly with that saying and would add that there's even more to life than the very good and fulfilling work that we hope you'll find in your dream job. Though our main focus has been to prepare you to find that dream job, we have an even deeper purpose for writing this book. That purpose is to help you live a good and fulfilling life—to get the whole life you want.

In this chapter, we invite you to explore what that whole life means for you. We'll begin by asking you to reflect on the people, things, and activities that you want to include in your life. Next, we'll ask you to delve a bit deeper and consider the underpinnings of your life—your values and beliefs, what we call your "philosophy of life." After that, we encourage you to look at those people you respect and admire—your role models—and consider how they can help you become the person you want to be. Finally, we'll invite you to look at your purpose or mission in life—what it is that you've been put on earth to do and who you are to become. In each of these areas, we'll ask you to spend time reflecting on different aspects of your life—how you want to live your life and what type of person you most want to be. Although you can learn from how other people answer these questions, to get the life you want, you must answer them with your own thoughts.

Envisioning Your Life, Defining Your Future

What kind of life do you want? Knowing what you want is the first step to making that life happen. As you've gone through this book, you've spent a lot of time discovering what it is you want in your dream job. But what else do you want? How do you want to fill your hours outside of work? What about being alive is most important to you? Here are a few things you might want as part of your whole life:

- Friends, family, a life partner, children, pets

- Sports and outdoor activities

- Cultural activities (theater, music, dance)

- Travel and time for hobbies

- Involvement with community or religious organizations

- Participation in political or environmental causes

Obviously, there are many more things you can do with your time outside work, but we hope this short list will be enough to get you thinking about what you want in your life. Another way of looking at it is to think about what you enjoy doing now and want to continue doing. Also consider whether anything is missing from your life that you want to be a part of your future.

> The power of vision is extraordinary.
>
> —DeWITT JONES, award-winning National Geographic photographer

For example, what kind of family life do you want to have as an adult, particularly in relation to your work? Will it be like the family life you have now, or will it be different? Kyle, age fifteen, wants something different because, as he puts it, "My dad hides out at work." Family life is often neglected these days. Parents now spend 40 percent less time with their children than they did in the 1960s. If you want to have children, what kind of parent do you want to be? What kind of family life do you want to have?

Lisa, age fifteen, also wants something different because, she says, "Sometimes adults make it seem like all they do is work. This doesn't make being an adult very attractive." What would make being an adult attractive to you? Who are the adults you admire—and why do you admire them?

The following exercise will help you envision your future and the way you want to live your life, including what and who you want to play a part in it. Pretend a magic wand has been waved over your life, giving you everything that's important to you in your ideal life. Have fun with this, but also give yourself plenty of time to

PICTURING YOUR IDEAL LIFE

To do this exercise, you'll need the following materials (or, if you have computer skills for doing graphic art, you may prefer to use your computer):

- A large piece of white paper
- Colored pencils or pens
- Old magazines that you can cut up
- Scissors
- Glue

Draw pictures or symbols, or create a collage to express visually the kind of life you want to live. Use the following questions to get yourself thinking about what you want to include in your picture (but be sure to add anything else that's important to you):

- In your ideal life, where do you live (city, suburb, rural area, on an island, in the mountains)?
- What kind of house or living space do you want?
- What is your neighborhood like?
- Who is with you (friends, family, pets)?
- What do you do for a living?
- Do you want to travel? Where do you want to go?
- Where do you want to vacation?
- What activities—sports, cultural, religious/spiritual, family, community—do you want to participate in?

You may want to work on your picture for several days until you feel it truly represents the life you want.

Now, look at your picture again. Take a few minutes to think about what you need to do to help make this ideal life happen. Because you can't do everything at once, choose one area that you can do something about now. (You may want to return to chapter 7 to review how to set short-term and long-term goals.) Having a vision of what you want your life to be is an important step in helping it become reality.

think about what matters most to you. You might want to complete this exercise over several days or even a few weeks to let what's really important to you rise to the surface. The goal is to have a visual image—a concrete vision—of your ideal life.

Once you have a concrete vision of your future, let's explore more deeply how you want to live that life and who you want to be. This includes discovering the unique contribution you have to make to the world and finding meaning in life—in your individual life and in the world around you. As you live, love, and learn more about life, you'll create—spoken or unspoken—a philosophy of life, a way in which you understand and view life events and people. A philosophy of

WRITING YOUR PHILOSOPHY OF LIFE

Everyone needs an "operating manual" for his or her life. That's really what a philosophy of life is. It identifies what you value most in life and articulates how you want to live your life. Your life philosophy will also guide your decisions.

Begin by writing down what is most important to you (for example, family, friends, money, art, freedom, or whatever). Think about why these are important to you and why you want them to be a part of your life. You may find that this exercise overlaps with the previous exercise—friends and family, for example, may come up in both exercises. That's fine. Now, go a bit further and think about particular qualities that are important to you, such as truth, integrity, peace, compassion, or forgiveness.

Next, list the beliefs by which you intend to live your life (for example, all people are created equal, creation is sacred, or love is more powerful than hate). Then think about how you'll face difficult times in your life. How do you hope you'll react to obstacles that may block the path to your goals? How will you deal with loss or frustration?

Give yourself time to think about what you value and believe. Think about what makes your life meaningful. Work on your philosophy of life for ten minutes a day for a week, or spend some time on it each weekend for a month or two. See what emerges as you reflect on these important matters. Your philosophy of life will evolve and grow as you do. Revisit the list of questions from time to time to think about what matters most to you.

If you hit a rough patch in life, reviewing your philosophy of life will help you assess what went wrong and how to get back on track. If you're ever disappointed with yourself or your life, ask yourself these questions:

- Am I paying attention to what I value most?
- Am I living my life by what I most deeply believe?

TIP: Get started thinking about your philosophy of life by watching Grammy winner John Legend giving a speech entitled Living a Soulful Life at **www.youtube.com/watch?v=NSIQszUAvow**.

life also helps you to interpret and understand your life experiences. For some, this meaning will be grounded in their religious or spiritual beliefs and the interaction of those beliefs with their life experiences; for others, it will grow more directly out of their life experiences. We invite you to take a few minutes now to reflect on your philosophy of life.

Your philosophy of life shapes everything that you do, as well as everything you are and are becoming. It shapes all aspects of your life. Just as you created a concrete vision of your future life in the discovery exercise Picturing Your Ideal Life, writing out your philosophy of life will help you articulate how you want to live your life. And, as we said before, knowing what you want is the first step to making it happen.

Becoming the Person You Want to Be

As you picture your ideal life and articulate your philosophy of life, you may also want to reflect on what kind of person you want to be. When you think about the person you want to be, you'll undoubtedly think about people who are important to you—people who have helped, inspired, befriended, or supported you through thick and thin. Who are the people you respect and admire? Who are your role models? Take a few moments now to reflect on those people who, by their lives and example, can help you become the person you want to be.

> Those who preserve their integrity remain unshaken by the storms of daily life. They do not stir like leaves on a tree or follow the herd where it runs. In their mind remains the ideal attitude and conduct of living. This is not something given to them by others. It is their roots. . . . It is a strength that exists deep within them.
>
> —ANONYMOUS

Reflecting on the traits you value— those that you most admire in the people you consider to be your role models— can help you cultivate those traits in your own life. If you can, arrange to talk with one or more of your role models about a trait of theirs that you particularly admire; for example, their compassion, intellect, wit, honesty, or ability to make people feel comfortable. Ask them how they developed that trait and who their role models were and are. See whether they have suggestions as to how you can develop that trait in your own life.

MY ROLE MODELS

Take a sheet of paper and turn it so that the long edge is horizontal. Fold the sheet in half, crease it, and then fold it in half again. You should have four columns of equal width.

Title the first column "Names of people I admire." Under that heading, make a list of people you admire. These can be real people you know or have known, historical figures, or fictional characters from books, movies, comic books, or TV.

Title the second column "What I admire about them or their lives." Think about each person in the first column, and then write down what you admire about them.

Title the third column "Do I have this trait?" Read over the traits you've written for each of the people you admire. Ask yourself, "Do I have this trait? Do I want to have this trait?" Write your answers in the third column.

Title the last column "How can I develop this trait?" Answer this question for each trait or attribute you'd like to develop or strengthen.

Discovering Your Mission in Life

You've been reflecting on very important aspects of your life—how you want to live your life, what you most deeply value and believe, and whom you most deeply admire. Your reflections on these questions, along with the other explorations you've made in this book, will help you find your purpose or mission in life—that is, what you are alive to do. Each of us has a purpose for being alive, and through pursuing our mission, we use our unique talents to contribute something to the

> Don't confuse life and work. It is much easier to write a resume than to craft a spirit.
>
> —ANNA QUINDLEN, writer

world, making it a better place to live, both for us now and for the generations that will follow us. There are three aspects to this mission:

1. Our lives are not simply to be filled with doing things; who we are and how we live our lives—our very being—is also important.

2. We are to do what we can do—moment by moment, day by day—to make this world a better place. In every situation, we each must do what we can to bring more gratitude, kindness, forgiveness, honesty, and love into the world.

3. Each of us must discover our purpose in life: how to use the talent that we came to earth to use. To do this, we each need to find and use our

greatest gift—the gift that delights us when we use it—in the places or with the people where we are drawn to use that gift and where it is most needed in the world.

As you seek your mission in life, always remember that you have something important to offer the world. The gift you are and the gifts you have to offer are unique. Only you can be you. Only you can fulfill your mission. Only you can give your unique gift to make the world a better place.

Our Wish for You

> Always be a first-rate version of yourself, instead of a second-rate version of somebody else.
>
> —JUDY GARLAND, singer and actress

As we close, we wish you well as you discover yourself, define your future, and live out your mission in life. Finding the job you want and creating the life you want can only be done by you. May you find work that challenges, satisfies, and delights you. May that work be part of a whole life that is good and fulfilling in every way. May you live out your life purpose—your mission—and give what only you can give to make the world a better place.

As you move from teen to adult, we hope you will: Tell the truth. Take some (manageable) risks. Be a bit cautious. Be thorough. Be persistent. Be kind. Become prepared to deal with the good and the disappointing parts of life. Live fully, love deeply, and always remember that step by step, day by day, you are creating your life and your future.

THE THREE Ms

The three Ms—mission, model, mirror—help you define what kind of character you are developing. Throughout your life, keep checking your growth by asking yourself these questions:

Mission: What is my purpose in life? How can I make the world a better place?

Model: Whom do I admire? Who are my role models? Who lives the kind of life I most want to live?

Mirror: Am I the kind of person I want to be?

APPENDIX A. WHAT EVERYONE WANTS TO KNOW: WHERE ARE THE JOBS?

In an ordinary recession, jobs are lost in a few sectors of the economy. In a severe recession, jobs are lost across all sectors of the economy. During the extraordinary recession of the past few years, the U.S. economy has lost over seven million jobs from all sectors.

Amazingly enough, in Fall 2009, there were also three million jobs vacant because employers can't fill them. The current openings are in technical, scientific, health-related, and government organizations. Why? Because employers can't find people with the skills needed for the jobs that are vacant. This discrepancy between the job skills people think they need and those sought by employers is yet another reason why postponing career exploration and decision making until after high school is not a strategy for success. You need time to *ascertain* (that's a PSAT and AP word) whether any of the jobs in demand can help you get your dream job. A majority of the jobs now vacant are high-skill, high-pay technical jobs. Since the advent of globalization, there is no such thing as just a U.S. job. If employers can't find U.S. citizens to fill vacant jobs, they will hire skilled applicants from other countries.

You have a choice of what to study, both in high school and afterward. When the economy is dicey and there are lots of people unemployed, students must determine which fields or jobs are in high demand that overlap their interests. This involves not only reading about various careers, but once again job shadowing and talking with employers to confirm employment possibilities and what type of training is available. Thousands of students have found that once they leave school, it is much easier to get into the workforce if they have training for jobs that are in high demand.

Authors' note: We are frequently asked, "Should students take into account jobs that are in demand or only pursue jobs they'll love?" In the last decade, students have been encouraged to figure out a career path based on what they really enjoy doing. That's better than the advice your parents and grandparents probably were given: "Just get a job, any job." Liking one's work wasn't considered important. In reality, that's not such good advice, because it's hard to become successful in a job you don't like. However, one factor has been overlooked, especially by academia: What's the demand for the jobs that most interest you? If demand is weak, what other jobs in greater demand are out there that use your skills and let you learn something interesting? With good research, students can probably find jobs that are in demand and that they will also love.

> We become happier, much happier, when we realize that life is an opportunity rather than an obligation.
>
> —MARY AUGUSTINE

Many of those three million job openings need people with STEM skills. *STEM* is an acronym for Science, Technology, Engineering, and Math. For years, employers at high-technology businesses have been asking schools to train more students in these fields. Unfortunately, fewer U.S. students have gained these skills, whereas students from other countries have continued to prepare for STEM careers. Most industrialized countries graduate more students with STEM skills than the United States does. These well-educated workers come to the United States for the high-skill, high-pay jobs that make up STEM careers.

STEM skills also drive business cycles. Think about the changes in the United States and the global economy due to the boom in the domestic auto industry during the 1950s and the decades following the birth of Silicon Valley's magic microchip. When a new business sector surges, millions of jobs are created directly or indirectly. American job creation lags when fewer elementary, secondary, and higher education students know basic scientific history and principles.

However, if quantum physics, inorganic chemistry, or advanced trigonometry are not your strongest subjects, please consider two things:

1. Weaknesses in math or science may mean you had teachers who weren't strong in these subjects either. If you are interested in exploring STEM careers, but not strong in math or science, find a good tutor, or take a remedial class or a class for people with math or science phobias. Most students have the ability to learn science and math, but not all students can learn them the same way. Students who don't get academic math, for example, may totally get it if the math is applied in ways that interest them.

2. Even if you aren't ever likely to be a techie, an area that is growing economically may have more job options for you. For example, a thriving high-tech corporation has dozens of nontechnical jobs. Whether it's in a state-of-the-art research hospital, a rocket manufacturer, or a multiblock computer campus, there are many nonscience jobs that require skills ranging from professional to labor at highly technical businesses. Someone writes marketing materials; maintains the financial records, roads, or landscaping; cleans the offices; does security; provides legal counsel; repairs the electricity or HVAC; runs the cafeteria; designs ergonomically efficient work spaces; and so on.

"Durable" is a word that is similar to "sustainable." When something is durable, it lasts for a long time without showing damage or wear. Students who obtain and keep adding to their STEM skills are likely to have very durable careers. Few can accurately predict the future. Based on the past, it is almost certain that new technologies needing STEM skills will keep emerging and will continue to drive the job market, the stock market, and the economy.

IF YOU WANT TO EXPLORE FURTHER...

STEM jobs and careers are in the news. Type "stem careers" into a search engine and you'll get dozens of links. Read a few recent ones and a few older ones to get a balance of information.

Two websites at which you can learn about STEM skills and careers are

www.bls.gov/opub/ooq/2007/spring/art04.pdf

www.stemcareer.com/

APPENDIX B. CONSIDERING COLLEGE?

As a high school junior or senior, you probably consider yourself a savvy consumer. When you buy something, you check out different stores for a bargain with the best features. You and your friends share tales of getting a good deal on recent purchases.

Do you know that a bachelor's degree can cost from $50,000 to over $120,000? A college education is likely to be the most expensive product you've ever bought.

To choose a college that's right for you, it's extremely important to apply your consumer smarts. To make a good decision, you need to know the following:

1. DO YOU NEED A DEGREE?

Additional education or training after high school is needed for 75 percent of today's jobs. Yet less than 25 percent of those jobs require college degrees. Of course, there are jobs for which a bachelor's degree is essential. Are you going for one of those jobs? Don't assume that a degree makes you more employable. If you are wrong, you've wasted tens of thousands of dollars and several years of your life. Talk with a half dozen people who are doing the work you want to do. Find out from them whether a college degree is necessary. If it is, they may suggest colleges that have exceptional departments or programs for what you need to study.

2. WHAT CAN YOU AFFORD?

Nationwide, only 32 percent of college students graduate in four years; 68 percent graduate in six years. If you need to work or can't get the right classes for graduation, you may spend more than four years getting an undergraduate degree. Stretch your money by going to a community college or less costly state college first and then transferring to complete your major. Even better, learn an in-demand trade that can support you and your studies without borrowing.

3. HOW CAN YOU AVOID OVERBORROWING?

The average grad has $25,000 in student loans and $4,100 charged on credit cards. Private loans can push debt load even higher. Limit your total borrowing to no more than two-thirds of your likely starting salary, or you won't be able to pay your bills. Being heavily in debt not only is stressful but also can limit your job and graduate school options.

4. WHICH SCHOOLS HAVE VALUE-ADDED PROGRAMS?

Employers hire candidates who can quickly become productive. Internships, co-op education, service learning, campus chapters of professional organizations, and study- and work-abroad experiences all increase your employability. If you want to work at a campus radio station, newspaper, or other cool position to add to your credentials, remember that these opportunities are much harder to get at big-name schools.

5. WHO HAS THE BEST SUPPORT PROGRAMS?

Being away from home is so exciting. It can also be overwhelming living 24-7 with strangers whose habits and values are so different from your own. Sharing a postage-stamp-sized room with someone is challenging. Look for schools with strong student or residential life programs that teach time management, setting priorities, study skills, and conflict resolution and that give an overview of leadership and team-building opportunities or clubs.

Also, check out career centers. If you haven't a clue what work you want to do after you graduate or you want to have a job before then, you'll need help from a competent career counselor.

APPENDIX C. MORE INFORMATION INTERVIEWS

CAREER ADVISER

Name: Megan Pittsley　　**Age:** 27
Job Title: Director of career services
Field(s): Education / human services
Employer: TechSkills San Jose
Degree(s): BS and AAS, management and public policy (concentration in human resources)
Cost: Unsure
Training: Global Career Development Facilitator Certificate
Cost: $600
Salary: Starting $40,000; three to six years' experience: $70,000

What do you do?
I assist graduates in finding employment. I provide career advising sessions, host workshops, arrange for special speakers, organize job fairs, instruct classes, and do lots of administrative tasks.

What are your most repetitive tasks?
I process lots of paperwork, but my job actually does provide a lot of variety.

Do you supervise anyone?
Not currently, but I will probably be hiring someone this year to support my department.

How long have you been at this job?
I just began this specific position, but I've been in the career advising, management, and recruiting field for about 9 years total.

How did you get into this work?
My first job advising people was in artist management, which I began right out of high school. I was very successful and one of the acts I managed even got on MTV. I then started working in staffing and human resources and decided to use my knowledge for the good of others. My first "real" career job was in a vocational college within the career services department.

What do you like about your work?
It's extremely rewarding. I make a difference in others' lives every day and empower them to be self-sufficient throughout their lives.

What don't you like about your job?
It can be very demanding and numbers-oriented because I need to make sure the school's graduates obtain employment. It's also sometimes discouraging when people really don't want to work or put in the required effort to get a job, or don't take my advice and thus stay out of work longer.

What are the main challenges in this industry?
It seems like a lot of people are trying to get into the career field now because of the bad economy. The ones who don't have the right experience and training are hurting job seekers and taking advantage of them; it can be very difficult to stand out amongst a heap of others searching for the same work.

What do you see happening in this field in the next 5 to 10 years?
Hopefully the field will slow down as the economy gets better and it will go back to being more regulated and ethical. It's a service that is always going to be needed because people will always need work!

Have you used social networking in a job search?
LinkedIn is a great site for professional social networking. Many other social networking sites are unprofessional and should be kept private if you use them for social purposes.

Did you have an internship in school? If yes, was it helpful to your employment?
I did have an internship in school, but it was really my work experience that was more valuable to my career. One unusual decision I made that has made all the difference in my career was that I worked full-time throughout my education, so I built my education at the same rate with my experience. It has proved invaluable for standing out against others my age.

What is your ultimate career goal?
I would like to work for a government-run career center in a management role and to create more innovative programs that will educate people about the changes the job market and job-search techniques have undergone in the last five years.

What advice would you give a young adult who wants to work in your field?
Get some experience in the staffing industry so you really know what makes candidates stand out and get hired. Learn the practical knowledge that will allow you to better assist your future career clients instead of just using what you learned in school. Volunteering at a local job club is also a great idea.

Outside your job, what are your other interests or hobbies?
I play on a roller derby team, and I enjoy gourmet cooking, kayaking, and camping.

Additional comments:
Don't be afraid to take risks and follow your passion. If you put in enough hard work, balanced with a practical approach to preparing yourself, you can succeed at anything!

Megan can be reached at Megan.Pittsley@ gmail.com, or you can visit her website at **www.meganpittsley.com**.

(HAZARDOUS) WASTE MANAGEMENT SPECIALIST

Name: Emily Wang   **Age:** 28
Job Title: Integrated waste management specialist
Field(s): Hazardous waste management; environmental policy
Employer: State integrated waste management board
Degree(s): BS, biology
Cost: $80,000 ($30,000 after grants and scholarships)
Training: Mostly on-the-job
Cost: None
Salary: Starting $37,000; three to six years' experience: $57,000–$68,000

What do you do?

I compile and analyze collection and cost data on various household hazardous waste (paint, used oil, mercury lamps) from local government agencies. I use this data to track statewide household hazardous waste trends and to identify areas that we can focus on to make our programs run more efficiently. The second part of my job is related to policy. I work with various stakeholders (local government, industry, and nonprofit organizations) to create new programs that will help with the future management of these wastes. This includes developing legislation, advising policymakers, and implementing new laws that are passed.

What are your most repetitive tasks?

I spend a lot of time compiling data and organizing it into charts and reports. The most repetitive task I have to do is double-checking and cleaning up data. I receive collection numbers from local government, but the data is not always given to me in the same format. I spend a lot of time going through and categorizing raw data, which means a lot of time spent going through Excel spreadsheets, making notes on each line. I must make sure everyone is using the same units, and also that there are consistent numbers being used when multiple sources are involved.

Do you supervise anyone? No.

How long have you been in this job?
Almost two years.

How did you get into this work?

I originally started out in the field of biochemistry research, but I found it to be unrewarding. So I took some time off, and worked as a construction consultant for a year. I applied for my job at the Waste Board because it provided a great opportunity to use my background in research to directly impact and benefit the environment, which has always been a passion of mine.

What do you like about your job?

I love that my job gives me a chance to directly impact the environment in a positive way. Performing my job well means that I am helping to keep millions of pounds of toxic chemicals out of landfills and leaching into groundwater. I also like that my job provides me with a wide variety of tasks and subject matter to study. One day I might be poring over data, while another day I could be on the phone with other states to discuss nationwide policy efforts, and the next I could be assisting a local government agency that is trying to build a new facility.

What don't you like about your job?

Part of my job relates to policy and legislation, and I find the political aspect of the legislative process rather opaque and frustrating. It is difficult to watch legislation sit in committee for reasons that have nothing to do with the merit or even the contents of the bill.

What are the main challenges in this industry?

There are two main challenges we are facing: collection levels and funding. Household hazardous waste management programs are primarily run by government programs at the city and county level. They collect less than 10 percent of the hazardous waste being generated, which means that there is still a huge amount of hazardous waste that is not being properly managed. While it is very encouraging that collection numbers have been increasing steadily, local government programs are becoming increasingly unable to support these programs financially. The problem of funding the management of these materials grows as the amount of these materials present in the environment grows.

What do you see happening in this field in the next five to ten years?

Traditionally, a manufacturer will make a product and sell it, and then it is up to the consumer to properly dispose of it when the product reaches the end of its life. This often means the product will end up in a landfill. Some products, like paint, consumers may realize should not be trashed and instead are taken to household hazardous waste facilities. Both the landfill and these facilities are mostly government run and operated sites. This means that the government (and by extension, the taxpayer) is the only entity financially responsible for managing these products at the end of their life. In the past few years, the idea of producer responsibility has been gaining a great deal of support. If a manufacturer is made to be in part responsible for the end-of-life management of their products, they are more likely to design products with less waste and fewer toxic materials. I expect to see multiple producer responsibility programs being implemented for various products around the country.

Have you used social networking in a job search?

No.

What is your ultimate career goal?

To keep working in my field and help to create meaningful environmental policies nationwide.

What advice would you give a young adult who wants to work in your field?

A solid science background is very useful, but building up connections to people who work in the field is even more invaluable.

Outside your job, what are your other interests or hobbies?

Scuba diving, rock climbing, reading, and wildlife conservation.

Additional comments:

It's very important to find a field you find both interesting and rewarding. While I find biochemical research to be fascinating, I find the process of the work itself to be very unrewarding and tedious, so ultimately it could not be satisfying.

Emily can be reached at emily.wang@calrecycle.ca.gov.

INFORMATION TECHNOLOGY MANAGER

Name: Nick Mitchell   **Age:** 25
Job Title: IT manager / project manager
Field(s): Information technology (private sector)
Employer: Marin IT, Inc.
Degree(s): BS and MS, information technology
Cost: MS $40,000
Training: Twelve levels of Microsoft certification, three levels of Cisco
Cost: $13,000
Salary: Starting $90,000–$110,000; three to six years' experience: $150,000–$180,000

What do you do?
Technology consultant, project manager, and engineer for both public and private sector companies throughout the California Bay Area.

What are your most repetitive tasks?
Project design, client relations, site installations, and managing the company's hosted services. (Marin IT manages customers' IT services like email, data backups, disaster recovery plans, Internet services, and wireless services. By using our services, companies don't need to hire in-house knowledge or resources to be able to get enterprise-level equipment or service on things like email, backups, and wireless.)

Do you supervise anyone?
I supervise three sales engineers and support technicians.

How long have you been at this job?
Two years.

How did you get into this work?
I started by taking classes in high school and developing an interest in how technology works and different ways to use it. The Internet and various Internet services were big at the time, and the way it all worked together was something that had me wanting to know more.

What do you like about your work?
Interacting with people and constantly adding to my knowledge base. There is always more to learn. I learn something new every day. I also love having the ability to be creative in finding solutions to problems.

What don't you like about your job?
At times I see people at a hard point of their day. They might be experiencing some issues or outages that can cost a lot of money.

What are the main challenges in this industry?
The main challenges are being better than the next person and separating yourself from the pack. The industry is very competitive and you must work very hard and constantly be on top of your game.

What do you see happening in this field in the next 5 to 10 years?
The sky is the limit and it's hard to predict exactly where it will go. That said, I could see it continuing toward completely integrated technology for our everyday personal and professional lives.

Have you used social networking in a job search?
No.

Did you have an internship in school? If yes, was it helpful to your employment?
I did an internship while I was in school at Empire, for Empire. I would stay after class and help professors with computer lab setups, lesson setup, and testing, or any other help the professors needed.

What is your ultimate career goal?
My ultimate career goal is to manage a group of creative and innovative staff members who are extremely passionate about what they do.

What advice would you give a young adult who wants to work in your field?
Be passionate about what you do, work hard at it every day, and approach each day with purpose. If you want a job in information technology, do internships to get your foot in

the door. Go the extra mile and do certifications for common programs. These are a big help in getting a job.

Outside your job, what are your other interests or hobbies?
Exercise, coaching youth sports, and auto racing.

Additional comments:
I love to learn. I'd be in school my whole life if it paid. Also, the impression that high schools give out—that you have to go to college to get a good job—is just wrong.

If someone has an interest in a certain field, they should look into trade schools. I checked out community colleges, but I liked the schedule at my trade school better. Classes were every day, Monday through Friday, from 8 a.m. to 3 p.m., year-round. I thought this made better use of my time than a regular college schedule.

Want to hear more? Visit **www.igot2know.com/index.php?videoid=760&partnerid=34** for an interview with Nick. He can be reached at nick@marinit.com.

ORGANIC FARM MANAGER

Name: Molly Bloom **Age:** 28
Job Title: CSA* manager
Field(s): Organic, sustainable agriculture
Employer: Eatwell Farm
Degree(s): BA, international studies, Macalester College
Cost: $100,000
Training: Two years of experience as an apprentice on organic farms. Apprenticeship compensation always included room and produce from the farm, plus a stipend (ranging from $250/month to $900/month).
Salary: Starting: $11/hour; three to six years' experience: $13.50/hour

* Community Supported Agriculture, most commonly called "CSA," is a growing, thirty-year-old movement in which organic farmers sell directly to consumers, forming a unique community and partnership with them. In a CSA, subscribers help support small, regional farms by paying in advance for fresh, organic produce delivered weekly (or, in our case, biweekly) throughout the season or year. Each farm organizes their CSA differently.

What do you do?
I serve as both an office manager for the farm and the go-to person for all CSA members. We have about 1,200 members, and I help them in any way I can, mostly by educating them about how to use the produce we send them and about general farming ideas. I also assist them with any issues that arise with their deliveries or subscription. I edit our weekly newsletter, adding recipes that utilize items we are sending our members on any given week and providing information about how to properly use and store their produce. I update our website and generally try to keep things running as smoothly and efficiently as possible.

What are your most repetitive tasks?
I answer the phone and respond to email during most of my workweek, in order to answer customers', or potential customers', questions. I also frequently print newsletters and fliers.

Do you supervise anyone?
I directly supervise one employee and co-manage three others.

How long have you been at this job?
Three years.

How did you get into this work?
I spent a summer during college working as an intern on a collective of small, organic farms in Washington State. I immediately fell in love with the work, the people, and the lifestyle. I returned to college, finished, and wandered around for a while before realizing that I really just want to farm. Before this job, I had no business experience. I took this job to learn the office side of farming, and it worked! I have learned a lot.

What do you like about your work?

I love teaching people how to integrate a seasonal, local diet into their busy lives.

What don't you like about your job?

It does get a bit repetitive, from week to week.

What are the main challenges in this industry?

Jobs are few and far between; most farmers work for themselves and have employees who stick around for years and years. Farming is a career in which it's notoriously difficult to make a living (though you'll likely not have to worry about food to feed your family!).

What do you see happening in this field in the next 5 to 10 years?

Sustainable/organic farming is definitely getting more popular. Consumers are learning more about organics and the benefits of buying from local growers, and I see this trend growing bigger and stronger over the next decade.

Have you used social networking in a job search?

Not yet!

What is your ultimate career goal?

One day, I want to own and run a small organic farm of my own.

What advice would you give a young adult who wants to work in your field?

I strongly recommend working as an intern or apprentice on an organic farm in your region of choice. Doing the work is the only way to learn whether or not it's something you'll enjoy. I suggest choosing a farm based on the structure of the internship/apprenticeship (what kind of compensation do you need, and is this farm going to accommodate your needs?), what the farm offers (are you interested in orchards? animal husbandry? vegetables? working at farmers' markets?), and where you want to live. Don't forget the importance of how you feel about the people who work there, too. Most farms ask interns and volunteers to work with them for a few days to make sure it's a good personality match. This is important for both the farmers and you. Don't take an internship that doesn't fill most of your needs (and if there are some pieces missing, make sure you are comfortable finding those pieces elsewhere).

Outside your job, what are your other interests or hobbies?

I love to read, hike, run, cook, garden, and travel. I also like preserving foods!

SOCIAL MEDIA SPECIALIST

Name: Dan Schawbel   **Age:** 26
Job Title: Social media specialist / personal branding expert, author of *Me 2.0*, speaker, blogger, syndicated columnist, and magazine publisher
Field(s): Technology / personal branding
Employer: EMC Corporation / self
Degree(s): BS, Marketing, Bentley University
Salary: At EMC Corporation: Starting: $46,000; three years' experience: $60,000

What do you do?

For EMC Corporation, my role as a social media specialist is to develop a social media strategy for the company, including using blogs, social networks, new media press releases, and online brand monitoring, as well as training employees on how to use and engage in the social media world. I work across several departments: human resources, public relations, and marketing, and I also support RSA, a division of EMC. Outside of EMC, I'm the author of *Me 2.0: Build a Powerful Brand to Achieve Career Success* (Kaplan), as well as the owner of two blogs, PersonalBrandingBlog.com and StudentBranding.com (a branding and career blog for students of all ages). I also publish *Personal Branding Magazine*, write columns for *BusinessWeek* and *Metro US*, speak at colleges and universities, and help individuals build their brands.

What are your most repetitive tasks?

The system I use every day to manage my professional life starts off in Google reader (a feed reader), where I soak in everything that is going on in my industry, including technology, trends, and ideas. I then take the blog posts or news articles and if some are noteworthy, I'll bookmark them on Delicious.com, tweet them, and maybe turn a few into a blog post. Each day, I skim through about five hundred feeds, organize them, share a selection of them, and use them for upcoming presentations, blog posts, or other materials. This way I stay relevant, remain influential and credible, and am able to grow my own brand.

Do you supervise anyone?

At EMC, I have no direct reports and my manager is the director of public relations. Outside of EMC, I have a team of writers and editors, including editors for both blogs and the magazine, and several columnists and freelance writers who write articles on occasion. I typically have at least one intern working with me at a given time.

How long have you been in this job?

I've been working as a social media specialist at EMC for two years, but I have been with the company in other roles, including product marketing and web support, since I graduated from college. Outside of work, I've been in the personal branding world since March 2007.

What do you like about your job?

For my EMC job, I was recruited based on the expertise I demonstrated outside of the company. Within the six months between March and August of 2007, I had launched a blog, an online TV show, a magazine, and an award dedicated to the concept of personal branding. *Fast Company* wrote about my efforts and through that visibility I was recruited internally by an EMC vice president to create the first social media position. Instead of being told what to do, I'm able to create my own projects and be trusted, based on my credibility, to

have free rein. I also like working with a variety of people, both inside and outside of EMC, who have different perspectives on social media and branding.

What don't you like about your job?

One of the biggest challenges for me is that I'm a natural-born entrepreneur and when you work at large companies (EMC has 40,000 people worldwide), you have to go through an approval process for almost every project. Also, I like creating products and websites from scratch and then marketing them. When you work at a large company, you're only permitted to handle one part of the operation because the rest is covered by other employees.

What do you see happening in this field in the next five to ten years?

This field will be more centralized within every organization, regardless of size and industry. Social media requires a lot of labor, strategy, commitment, and support. Companies in the next few years will have to get engaged online if they want to compete, so this field is going to grow rapidly and there will be a lot of opportunities for people. It will evolve in the future as technology rapidly changes and there are new methods of communication to choose from.

What is your ultimate career goal?

I want to create an online university around personal branding, write more books, and have complete career freedom. I'm not looking to make millions of dollars like most professionals my age hope for. Instead, I'm positioning myself so that I can make money doing what I love, while having the flexibility and enjoyment of working whenever I want.

What advice would you give a young person who wanted to go into your field?

Any job that seems cool is very competitive and you can't even apply for the best jobs in the world. In order to counter this, you should invest your time in building a blog around your passion. If you build your blog around your passion, it will enable you to work hard enough to become the expert that companies will crave. By leveraging a blog and other social networks, you can gain enough visibility to be recruited for the job you want. The reason why this happens is because your personal brand will filter out all the jobs you don't want and attract the ones you do want. This wasn't possible five years ago, but now anyone who is committed enough to their career can accomplish it.

Other interests

My work is my life and I'm building my personal brand around a community that supports it. I enjoy running social events, writing, running, Boston nightlife, tennis, all kinds of music, and sports cars.

Additional comments

When I was in college, I disregarded networking because I was an introvert and uncomfortable with those types of situations. The result was an eight-month job hunt! The most valuable lesson I've learned throughout my life is to network before you need it. Most people network when they need a job so they are beggars. Instead, think about networking as life and try and meet the right people who can help you grow.

I would also consider working for a brand-name company when you graduate from college because people are familiar with it and it will make you a more attractive candidate in the future. I had eight internships during college, such as one with Reebok. Even though I didn't gain much experience at Reebok, during all of my interviews, the hiring manager always asked me about it over the lesser-known firms I had worked for.

Dan can be reached at dan.schawbel@gmail.com.

SOLAR ENERGY SALES COORDINATOR

Name: Evan Sarkisian   **Age:** 24
Job Title: Sales operations coordinator
Field(s): Alternative energy / sales / administration
Employer: REC Solar, Inc.
Degree(s): BA, philosophy (minor in general business), Santa Clara University
Training: Training comes in stages. As you take on more responsibilities you receive more training. I've taken training courses both in person and online.
Cost: Not sure. The more work-related the skill training is, the more likely my employer will pay for it. When I want to study something that probably won't directly impact my work performance, then I usually just go out and do it myself.
Salary: Starting: $34,000–$39,000; three to six years' experience: $40,000–$55,000+ (from Payscale.com)

What do you do?

I support the sales team's operational functions, ensuring quality and efficiency between our sales team and our implementation team. This includes contract administration, database management, and workflow process updates

What are your most repetitive tasks?

Contract review, project entry (Oracle Database), and creation of change orders (which are legal documents to change equipment or pricing structure for jobs).

Do you supervise anyone?

No, but I have trained people.

How long have you been at this job?

1 1/2 years.

How did you get into this work?

I was a member of the Santa Clara University Solar Decathlon team where I gained experience with the solar industry and working in teams. When I graduated I only applied to solar companies because I knew it was the right industry for me.

What do you like about your work?
The people I work with are intelligent, honest, and hardworking. It is a pleasure to learn from them and help them bring solar energy to the mainstream. I also enjoy being the focal point where our sales team meets our implementation team. It is a dynamic and challenging role, especially as this industry and company experience impressive growth; there is a lot of change over time.

What don't you like about your job?
Paperwork! But that's probably a pretty common complaint.

What are the main challenges in this industry?
Driving costs down and allocating resources to where they are needed most. As we grow it is hard to predict which areas of our business are going to be bottlenecks, and sometimes our only option is to work reactively to get resources to where they need to be (e.g., engineering or interconnection).

What do you see happening in this field in the next 5 to 10 years?
It is really hard to predict because our industry is so young and, like all energy, heavily dependent on government policy. My feeling is that we are poised for a lot of growth and we will see solar become cost-competitive in more areas around the world. This will drastically change the competitive landscape and the opportunities for work will increase.

Have you used social networking in a job search?
Yes, my school has a social networking site where you can find alumni in different industries. I contacted a few people who were from my school but they were in companies that needed engineers, which I am not.

Did you have an internship in school? If so, was it helpful to your employment?
The Solar Decathlon was similar to an internship. It was an international competition between twenty university teams to build an 800-square-foot solar-powered home. I was a member of the Communications Team for Santa Clara University's entry into the competition. It was definitely helpful. In interviews, I was able to describe the skills I have that could help the companies I was interviewing with, and I also demonstrated my interest in the industry.

What is your ultimate career goal?
I don't have a specific goal so much as a guiding principle. I want to apply my skills to their fullest extent in the pursuit of a low-carbon economy. I see the skills I have and look for opportunities, short- and long-term, where I can continue to apply and develop them in more deep and meaningful ways.

What advice would you give a young adult who wants to work in your field?
First, don't be afraid to open up to people you meet or already know about your interest in solar and finding a job in the field. For me, the best opportunities came during conversations with friends and family when I was talking about my job search. In fact, I got in contact with REC Solar because I complained to a friend about an interview with another solar company and how rude they were. My friend said she knew someone at REC. After that I was on my way to landing this job. Next, I also recommend getting involved in anything applicable to the industry on your own time. A lot of it can be fun, like volunteering on a solar project or making solar the topic of a research paper.

Outside your job, what are your other interests or hobbies?
Improvisation comedy, playing drums, continuing my education, and video games.

Evan can be reached at esarkisian@recsolar .com.

ABOUT THE AUTHORS

A career strategist since 1979, **CAROL CHRISTEN** has provided life/work planning and job-search skill training to individuals and groups, specializing in working with teenagers using the internationally renowned techniques found in *What Color Is Your Parachute?* From her research for the latest edition of this book, Carol has become convinced that to achieve career maturity and good grades, the career-search process for teens must start earlier; since it takes about a decade for young adults to go from clueless to well employed, why not start the process at fifteen? She continually asks the question, "Is there a downside to planning?" Carol lives with her husband on a small farm on California's Central Coast, where they raise colorful flowers and colorful chickens that lay lots of colorful eggs. You can contact her through her website, www.carolchristen.com.

RICHARD N. BOLLES has been a leader and the #1 celebrity in the career development field for more than thirty-five years. He was trained in chemical engineering at M.I.T.; in physics at Harvard University, where he graduated cum laude; and in New Testament studies at the General Theological (Episcopal) Seminary in New York City, where he earned a master's degree. He is the recipient of two honorary doctorates, is a member of MENSA, and is listed in *Who's Who in America* and *Who's Who in the World*. He lives in the San Francisco Bay Area with his wife, Marci. You can contact him through his website, www.jobhuntersbible.com.

JEAN M. BLOMQUIST is a freelance editor and writer with experience as a college admissions counselor.

INDEX

part-time, 60, 73
rating, 48–50
STEM, 160–61
summer, 60
vacant, 125, 159
Job search
advisory board for, 129
developing skills for, 61–62
effectiveness rate of, by method, 123
essentials for, 122–24
finances and, 144
as a full-time job, 124–25, 143
giving up on, 144–45
help in, 146
learning about, 143
length of, 125, 142, 144
luck and, 125
mentors for, 143
multiple targets in, 120, 121–22,
   145
techniques for, 142
time spent on, 142, 143
tips for, 124–29
unending nature of, 137
Job shadowing, 63–64, 78, 89

L

Life
envisioning ideal, 153–55
mission in, 157–58
philosophy of, 155–56
LinkedIn, 104, 105, 124
Luck, role of, 125

M

Mental skills, 11–12, 17
Mentors, 64, 78, 139, 140, 143
Mirror Theory, 25
Mission in life, 157–58
Mistakes, most common, 141–46

N

National Job Shadow Coalition, 63–64
Nemko, Marty, 48

Networking
benefits of, 42–43
contacts and, 117–18, 119
definition of, 42
green career sites for, 151
informal vs. formal, 42
social media sites for, 99–106, 121

O

Organizations
researching, 119–20
small, 126–27
targeting, 120, 121–22, 126–27

P

Parachute, image of, 6–7
Parachute diagram
blank, v
filling in, 19, 20, 25, 35, 37,
   38–39, 96
Part-time work, 60, 73
Party exercise, 23–25, 26, 27
Peace Corps, 73
People
favorite types of, 22–25, 27
researching, 104, 114
skills with, 12, 18, 86–87
Persistence, importance of, 144–45
Physical skills, 11, 16
Pitch, practicing, 126
Prioritizing, 21

R

References, 127
Research
on organizations, 119–20
on people, 104, 114
Resumes
lack of effectiveness of, 128
online, 104–5
updating, 147
Role models, 156–57, 158

S

Salary
  ideal, 34–35
  information on, 34, 140
  of recent college graduates, 82
Self-Directed Search (SDS), 27
Skills
  communication, 85
  definition of, 11
  desired by employers, 84–88
  enjoyable, 10–11
  identifying, 12–15, 19–21
  interests and, 10
  interpersonal (with people), 12, 18,
    86–87
  job-search, 61–62
  mental (with information), 11–12, 17
  physical (with things), 11, 16
  self-management (personal traits),
    20–21
  specific knowledge (work content), 20
  STEM, 160–61
  teamwork, 86
  transferable (functional), 11–14, 19, 20
Skill TIPs, 12, 14–20
Social entrepreneurs, 52
Social networking sites
  with a business focus, 104–5
  career exploration through, 101
  characteristics of, 99
  possibilities of, 106
  safety and, 100, 121
  Twitter, 103
  types of, 99–100
Start-up metaphor, 90–91
State Conservation Corps, 73
STEM skills, 160–61
Student loans, 82–83, 84
Study abroad, 53
Summer work, 60
Sustainability, 149–51

T

Teamwork skills, 86
Tech Prep classes, 70–71
Telephone calls
  best times for, 124
  number of, 125
  tips for, 125–26
  voice mail, 123–24
Thank-you notes, 50–51, 117, 136–37
To-do lists, 96–97
Traits, personal, 20–21
Twitter, 103

V

Vacancies, 125, 159
Voice mail, 123–24
Volunteer work, 79, 127–28

W

Web. *See also* Social networking sites
  creating a presence on, 102–3
  resumes on, 104–5
Work environment, ideal, 28–32, 35
Work ethic, 87–88